Acknowledgements

I would like to thank and acknowledge all the help I have been given over the last two years. Two people especially have helped enormously with this book. The first is Tony whose idea this book was and his input, particularly into the finds chapter which was enormous, as was his help with the overall style throughout the book.

The second is Micky who must also be mentioned. Her sketches, illustrations and line drawings of finds are first class and provide the informal and amusing flair that I was looking for. Also for her input into the proof reading - she managed to correct my writing into readable English!

There are a few others like Sam at the British Museum; Nigel and Gordon from our club who read the proofs, and corrected any slip-ups. Any mistakes that are still there are mine completely. If you find any, please feel free to let us know so we can correct them on the first reprint.

I would also like to acknowledge and thank the following photographers for the use of their photographs.

- The Trustees of the British Museum and the Portable Antiquities Scheme (PAS).
- Mike Hogan, who provided one of the photos of the Frome coins, and the one of Dr. Alice Roberts and me.
- Steve Minnitt, the director of Somerset Museum service who kindly provided the Frome hoard display layout in the Taunton Museum.
- Neil, a Somerset farmer, who provided a photo of himself and his cows.

Dave Crisp 2018

Editor
Greg Payne

Design Editor & Origination
Christine Jennett

Published by
Greenlight Publishing
The Publishing House, 119a Newland Street, Witham, Essex CM8 1WF
Tel: 01376 521900

info@greenlightpublishing.co.uk
www.greenlightpublishing.co.uk

Printed in Great Britain

ISBN 978 1 897738 47 4

Contents

		Page
	Introduction	4
1	Brief History of Metal Detectors and Our Hobby	5
2	Equipment	10
3	Starter Detectors On Test	18
4	Organisations, Clubs and Dealers	25
5	Where To Search and Ten Ways To Gain Permission	29
6	The Dangers of the Farm	42
7	Detecting Land	52
8	How To Detect	60
9	What You Can Find – Coins	69
10	What You Can Find – Artefacts	84
11	Portable Antiquities and Treasure	118
12	Cleaning, Conserving and Researching Finds	125
13	Upgrading to a More Expensive Machine	134
14	Not One Hoard, But Two!	138

Appendices

1	The Treasure Act	173
2	The National Council for Metal Detecting	174
3	Further Reading	176
4	Useful Contacts	178
5	Grid References	180

Introduction

Dave Crisp

My detecting partner Tony and I both started from scratch with no knowledge of metal detecting whatsoever. But between us we now have over 25 years' of experience.

It was in July 2010, after I had found the Frome Hoard of Roman coins, that Tony realised that there was limited information (in terms of books) for newcomers to the hobby to buy that would tell them what they needed to know. So he put it to me that we could put together an essential book on metal detecting, with all the relevant information, including the Portable Antiquities Scheme (PAS) and the1996 Treasure Act. This would also give me an opportunity to tell my story as finder of the Frome Hoard.

We are sure that you will find in this book the knowledge that you need to start the hobby correctly. Also covered is where to go, and how to use your detector. You will also see a selection of finds to help on initial identification of the objects you recover. There is a section on the 1996 Treasure Act and the Portable Antiquities Scheme where, through your local Finds Liaison Officers (FLOs), you can get help with the identification of finds. We have tried to make this a light-hearted look at our hobby and how to go about it, but with a look at the serious side of doing things correctly.

Throughout this book we have tried to emphasise the benefits of cooperation between museums, the archaeologists involved in the Portable Antiquities Scheme and detectorists.

We have also been very lucky to have comments and contributions from academics such as Roger Bland (head of PAS at the British Museum); Steve Minnet (Head of Somerset's Museum Service), and Katie Hinds (the FLO for Wiltshire). We are also indebted to Pippa Pearce for help on the conservation of finds, and Sam Moorhead (Iron Age and Roman Finds Advisor at the British Museum).

Good luck and good detecting - Dave Crisp

Brief History of Metal Detectors and Our Hobby

What is a Metal Detector?

A metal detector emits an electromagnetic field from its search coil. When a metal object enters this field it causes a change or distortion. This is relayed to the control box, which analyses the response and provides a sound in the operator's headphones and, on some models, a display on a screen. The strength and type of the signal can also tell the detector how deep the item is, and the type of metal it is made from. This information can also be displayed on some detectors.

One of the first detectors was built by an engineer by the name of Gerhard Fisher. In the late 1920s he was working on radio direction finding equipment for aircraft and found that metal ore in the ground, or metal roofs on buildings, affected the system. From this early beginning he designed a metal detector, for which he received a patent in 1937. These very early machines were also used by geologists, gas and electricity companies, and the police. During the Second World War and afterwards they also helped to clear enemy minefields. These early mine detectors were heavy and used a lot of power, but they were the cutting edge of technology at the time.

Lt. Jozef Kozacki designed the first practical electronic mine detector, called the "Mine Detector Polish Mark 1". It was soon improved upon and mass produced. Some 500 were issued to the British Army in time for use prior to the Battle of El Alamein in October 1942. An example is shown here (reproduced with permission). It looks quite familiar to a 21st century detectorist!

Second World War, 1942, mine detector.

My first BFO metal detector from the late 1960s.

After the war these very early machines were used at the very start of our hobby, although in those days you needed a partner just to carry the battery pack! It was in the 1950s and 1960s, with the invention of the transistor, that detectors transformed into lighter machines which used batteries that could be fitted integrally. In America, Charles Garrett obtained a patent for a "Beat Frequency Oscillator" type metal detector and this is when the hobby really started up, with more and more manufacturers coming into the market. Garrett was joined in the 1960s by other now well-known names such as White's and Fisher.

Shown above right is the first detector I ever purchased in the late 1960s. As you can see, it's just a hoop on a stick with an adapted transistor radio; but it still works (after a fashion!). It is tuned by using the slider on the main stem. I was assured, by the shop assistant that I would find lots of things with it! After a couple of outings in the garden it went into the cupboard, and has seen many more cupboards since then. I now bring it out as a curiosity when giving talks!

Tesoro, who started in the late 70s, became one of the early makers of a full range of machines. One of these models was the legendary, Silver Sabre, renowned for its ability to find small hammered coins. Tesoro, which is Spanish for treasure, are still going and I still use my Laser B1 as a backup machine.

Great strides at that time were also being made in improving coil design, important for depth and signal recognition. Induction Balance machines gave the opportunity to discriminate between metals and ignore the targets you did not want (iron). So with the ability to read the type of metal found, machines were getting more sophisticated. Also, with further improvements in discrimination, they were going forward in leaps and bounds.

One of the main bugbears of the early detectors was the effect on them of minerals in the ground. Reducing the effects of this mineralisation was one of the next big advances. However, manufacturers had to be careful in the design of this "ground balance" as some metals give similar readings to ground minerals, and if the facility is wrongly set some desirable objects could be lost and the detector suffer from loss of sensitivity.

Many new designs of coils came out in the mid to late 1970s, and this led to the development of "motion detectors". With these, by keeping the coil moving, the detector could discriminate and at the same time auto tune out the effects of ground mineralisation. By the 1980s and 1990s computer technology was incorporated into detector design, and this had a fantastic effect on the models available.

My Minelab Explorer II detector and the Roman hoard I found with it.

So we move into the late 1990s and the 21st century. What fantastic advances there were! Technology was advancing very quickly and giving us machines that were never dreamt of years ago. Many of the old names - such as Garrett, White's, Fisher, and Tesoro - are still producing excellent machines. However, they have been joined by others - notably Minelab that started in 1985 but now, in our view, produces some of the most advanced detectors available. It was the Minelab Explorer II that found the Frome Hoard!

The National Council for Metal Detecting (NCMD) was formed in 1981 in the dark days when most academics (archaeologists, museum curators etc.) did not get on with us, nor we with them. The archaeological community saw detectorists as little more than thieves, raiding important sites and destroying information. The detectorists saw the archaeologists as arrogant and untrustworthy, trying to keep the past to themselves. There were even moves to make the hobby illegal. Yet there were small pockets of enlightened people and individuals who recognised, early on, that we could provide a lot of information from objects we found that were not being recorded. So although most of the academics, working in museums, would have nothing to do with detectorists slowly, in some places, the views began to change.

The NCMD worked tirelessly to put across a reasoned and balanced view and argued that we should all be working together, for everyone's benefit. Some metal detectorists and museum curators realised that it was indeed possible to work together and to respect one another's views. One of the first places this happened was In Norfolk where archaeologist Tony Gregory (sadly now passed on) helped to improve relations and keep the dialogue going.

The NCMD were actively involved in the shaping of the 1996 Treasure Act (which came into force in 1997), and they are still democratically elected to represent the hobby. The NCMD have always had a code of conduct that members keep to, and in the back of the book is a copy that has been agreed by all the main parties involved. Trevor Austin, who is presently the Chairman, even sits on the Treasure Valuation Committee, which independently values items of Treasure. In my opinion, we would not have this great hobby today if it had not been for the National Council; with this organisation hobby metal detecting could have been banned or severely restricted.

Today we therefore have a hobby which is stronger, and attracts more interest from beginners, than ever before. The relationship between academics and detectorists has been transformed; indeed often the younger generation, on both sides, have no idea there was ever a problem.

Below is an example of today's cooperation between metal detectorists, museums, archaeologists, and the Portable Antiquities Scheme.

Coins On PAS Database

All the objects recorded by the staff of the Scheme are published on an online database, http://finds.org.uk, which (at the time of writing) contains records of some 725,000 objects, although this grows monthly. We also encourage finders with the right knowledge to record their finds on the database themselves. This unique resource does not exist anywhere else in the world and since 2003 around 18 000 people have volunteered finds for recording and/or participated in archaeological excavation/survey and finds recording. PAS data has increased the number of known Roman sites in Warwickshire and Worcestershire by over 30%, and more than doubled the number of known archaeological sites in Lincolnshire.

Of the 725,000 objects recorded by the scheme (at the time of writing), around 271 000 are coins. They break down as follows:

Iron Age	**42,361**	**(incorporating much of the Celtic Coin Index)**
Roman	**174,662**	**(incorporating Welsh data)**
Greek and Roman Provincial	**172**	
Byzantine	**97**	
Early Medieval	**2,443**	
Medieval	**29,198**	
Post-Medieval	**24,100**	
Modern	**216**	
Foreign	**119**	
Unspecified	**398**	
Total:	**271,066**	

(Data provided by Roger Bland and Sam Moorhead of the British Museum.)

Equipment

Congratulations! At this stage of reading my book you have now bought, or are thinking about buying, a metal detector. But what else do you need and what, more importantly, don't you need? Like any hobby, it's too easy to buy, or get sold, something you will never use. So let's look at a basic list of things that are going to make your detecting day a lot better and your research afterwards more enjoyable.

Detector

I hope that this book is going to help you choose a detector that will give you a good start in our hobby. However, your first choice is so important that I have allocated a complete chapter to just picking a suitable machine. As this isn't it, let's move on to other equipment.

Small Pinpoint Probe

A small pinpoint probe is one of the most useful bits of equipment that you can carry. You can live without one, but in my view it is worth getting a slightly cheaper detector and coughing up the £60 to £80 needed to buy one. They are little detectors in their own right and their job is to check the inside of your hole, or your pile of dirt, for the target you are digging. They can save you lots of time and frustration, and locate objects that you would otherwise lose. I have heard many detectorists' sad tales of ruined finds by them not realising that the item was just where they put in the spade for the second time. I would not be without mine, and it's about 18 years old now. All the writing has worn off, and it's held together by gaffer tape. I don't even know what make it is, but it's worth its weight in hammered silver to me. I carry it in a holster on my belt, with my knife, rubbish pouch, and a small first aid pack.

Small pinpoint probe.

Digger

Small spade used for farmland searches.

I once heard a story of a detectorist who gained permission to search a field but, on his first visit, was chased off by an irate lady shouting. "I didn't know you were going to dig holes!" You really can't do without one of these essential items and they come in many shapes and sizes, from small hand trowels to a garden spade that a navvy would be proud of. They are normally made of iron or stainless steel, either with the head welded to the shaft or made all in one.

A garden trowel is far from ideal as you would have to spend a lot of time stooping down, and it may well lack the strength. A large garden spade is too big and too heavy to cart around for hours on end. What you need is something that you can dig a hole with at just the correct size that you want. So it stands to reason that you need a sharp implement that will do the job and will not leave you with a hole the size of a grave. There are many purpose-made diggers on the market. You will find these for sale in *Treasure Hunting*, and from the detector dealers. The stainless steel ones are always going to be dearer, but they are stronger and much less inclined to break, so should last for many years.

The ideal size for the blade is about 4 inches across, and about 5-6 inches high, with a good long handle of about 24 inches. Some people lengthen the standard handle by adding a longer one and this will certainly help if you have a bad back. I use a small (and I mean small) 6 inches by 8 inches "lady's spade". As I now in my declining years, I find it's easier to carry and dig with this than some of the purpose made diggers.

Whatever you use, you will find it easier to dig in grass if the blade is kept sharp and I keep mine this way by running a sharpening stone over it most weeks. A good suitable digger can make all the difference to whether you enjoy the hobby or find it hard work. The standard garden trowel, as stated, is only really good for planting petunias.

Assorted diggers for various search conditions.

Headphones

Headphones should always be used as they enable you to hear the faint signals, rather than just the loud and medium ones (should you detector have an integral speaker).

Also, detecting without them is inconsiderate as internal speakers make a racket that disturbs other detectorists, the public, dogs, or just the tranquillity of the local countryside. The purchase of a good pair of headphones is a well worth the investment. There are many on the market, ranging from just a few pounds to well over £50. I think it's always wise to buy the best that you can afford, without breaking the bank. A quality pair of headphones will have a good layer of padding on them and perhaps a separate headphones-to-detector lead. (In the past my lead always seemed to break at the detector end by the jack-plug). Some manufactures (i.e. Minelab), provide a well-suited pair of headphones matched to a specific detector to obtain best results.

Belt Pouches

A pouch that has a few different compartments is very handy as you don't want your good finds mixed up with the dross. A few small plastic bags are very useful for small good finds. Also on my belt I have a long blunt knife that is very practical for finding items when the probe says they are in the side of the hole. In a small pack on the back of the belt I carry a plastic rain poncho and a small first aid tin. Both of these items I have never had to use, but as the Scouts say: "Be prepared".

Gloves

These are always a personal issue; I always wear them but I know of many detectorists who never do. The way I look at it, is to just think of what has gone into the soil over the years: cows, sheep and horses have all done their thing, and in the Victorian age all the night soil from the towns was spread across it. The farmers have dosed the fields with every known chemical they can think of and a few more, just to make the crops grow, and that's just the start. Then you have all the sharp bits of tin cans, barbed wire, and items that would look good on an alien spacecraft. Next you have all the items of rubbish, some of which can be very sharp, including discarded needles from the old time vets, which quite regularly turn up and then, my favourite, the screw bottle top which gives such a good signal, but also has an inch of broken glass still attached to it. Even a blade of maize can give you a nasty cut, which can get infected. A good pair of leather gloves will set you back a few pounds in a garden centre, but keep you warm in the winter and will last years; they are well worth it in my opinion.

Footwear

I always start out in a pair of boots and only put my Wellingtons on if it is really necessary. Some people wear normal shoes, even trainers, but a pair of boots comes in handy when walking or detecting across stubble fields. When out detecting you can encounter stone or muddy tracks, boggy fields, stubble, brambles and stinging nettles, or a rough ploughed field that can take on the feel of a Himalayan trek.

I still remember the day when I wore a pair of steel toecap boots – never a good idea although I got plenty of signals! I had to spend one of the hottest days of the year wearing my Wellingtons while other people were in shorts and trainers. I provided a few laughs that day but, since then, I always double check before I leave. A pair of Wellingtons is a must if you want to keep your feet warm and dry. These are not a fantastic expense and, with a second pair of socks on, walking on wet winter fields does not have to be like walking on blocks of ice.

Maps

I find a small map of the fields I am detecting in very useful, as this not only shows you where you are, but also where you want to go. It also allows you to plot your find spots, as you might not remember where each item came from when you get home. A copy of a map can help the landowner mark where you can go on his land. He might also be able to point out fields which belong to other farmers and that's always very useful. A GPS system can be used to plot your find spots very accurately, but there is quite a price tag (although they are getting cheaper), which might not be cost effective for somebody just starting out in the hobby.

Extra batteries

A pack of spare batteries in the car can save the day sometimes, because wherever you go it's not going to have a shop in the corner of the field and, even if it did, they wouldn't stock the ones you need. If it's not you, then they might come in handy for somebody else. I remember saving the day for somebody at a rally (who will remain nameless) by giving him a brand new pack. At the end of a long day, he took them out of his detector and gave them back to me: it's a funny old world!

There are two basic types to use: disposable or rechargeable. Alkaline disposables are relatively cheap, but you have to keep buying more. Good lithium rechargeable batteries are dear to buy, and you have to include the price of the charger in the total; but you can recharge them at least 300 times, according to the pack. A good set of batteries normally last me for two full days' detecting. You can buy the cheap and cheerful ones from your local supermarket, but a quality set seem to last a lot longer - and do you really want to be detecting when your machine is working only on half power?

Clothing

You are definitely, at some stage, going to need a windproof coat and a warm hat as it can get quite cold in the fields in late summer and even worse in winter. A good coat will keep out the cold and keep you dry if you are caught out in a rain shower. With a hat, which can be stuffed in a pocket or rucksack, you will keep your head warm, and that is a must in winter. A pair of headphones will keep your ears warm, but that's about all. Both coat and hat can be utilised from normal clothing, and don't have to be bought specifically. I keep a pair of waterproof over-trousers in my car, just in case it's windy and cold on a winter's day.

Kneepads

As you get older these might come in useful, I personally cannot get on with them, and just have a cut down kneeling pad on a bit of elastic string fixed to my belt. It works for me.

FIRST AID

Small Rucksack

Personally I don't bother with a rucksack but I know that my detecting partner Tony does. He crams it full of hats, anoraks, compasses, water, sandwiches and spare batteries. Each to their own, I suppose. Oh yes, and a small first aid kit which, I guess, is quite a good idea.

Chair & Lunch

A small folding chair carried in the car, will be a welcoming item for food breaks. As you get on in years, there is nothing more pleasing than a chair to sit on when you have your lunch ("What a sad comment on old age, Dave!" as Tony would say). A chair takes the weight off your legs for 10 minutes or so, and gives you a new burst of energy to start again. Always carry something to eat and drink, as you never know when you will need it. Even just some chocolate and a can of drink can make all the difference.

Grid Position System

The one piece of equipment that we have not talked about is a handheld GPS. Why do we need one of these you might say? Well you don't, unless you want to know exactly where you found an item next week, next year or in 10 years time and return to a "hot spot". A GPS reference for your find is as accurate as you can get.

If you are going to record your interesting finds with your FLO then they would prefer a six or eight figure grid reference, but they will accept just a parish reference.

If you are of the old school, as I am, you will be aware that you can fix your position in a field quite accurately with only a Ordnance Survey map, a piece of card and a pencil. This will pinpoint your find down to an area 100 metres square. An "ABC" of how to take a simple map reference is given at the back of the book.

I personally do not yet use a GPS system and, to my knowledge, there is only one person in our club of 50 members who does; so they are not yet standard equipment for detectorists. What will this little piece of kit cost you? Well, you can get a small basic device that you can carry in your pocket for about £60-£80. (In reality, this could be only the cost of a good night out for two with a curry to finish!)

But perhaps, unless you like gadgets, you might not need one of these GPS machines; you can do the same thing with your map, a pencil, and a piece of card. (You will find easy-to-use instructions later in this book).

There is a second "high tech" option, and that is using one of the Web Maps provided by organisations like Google in conjunction with Ordnance Survey, where you can find where you were detecting, and just read off the grid reference (http://wtp2.appspot.com/wheresthepath.htm)

You will have two screens: on the left an Ordnance Survey map, on the right a Google satellite image. Just drag the map to where you want it, and zoom in! You will then have two sets of five numbers. Write down the first three numbers of each from the left, add the two letters that are there, and you have a six figure map reference (i.e. ST 742489).

There is a second web site in the appendences at the back, so there are three ways to record a grid reference.

Final List

So we seem to have all the items necessary to go detecting, or do we? Perhaps we need just a little more?

- Tent
- Spare digger
- Pack horse to carry it all
- A large trailer
- Extra wet weather clothing
- Spare detector
- A 4x4 all-terrain vehicle

Always carry extra wet weather gear just in case you get wet; also a tent is useful if you get a bit tired. What about a spare digger in case your one breaks, and another detector for emergencies? With all this gear a pack horse might come in useful with a trailer in case he gets tired. And last a 4x4 all-terrain vehicle to pull the trailer. Well, perhaps not!

Do you need all of the (sensible) kit? The answer is no, as all you need is a detector and something to dig with, but the rest of the bits will make your day more enjoyable and you will have the satisfaction of knowing you can go out detecting, and are ready as can be, for whatever occurs.

NO KITCHEN SINK

Starter Detectors On Test

Let's talk detectors! This is the item on the top of your shopping list and the one that is most essential - and most expensive - for your new hobby. Like cars metal detectors come in all shapes, sizes and budgets; you can buy one new for as little as £50 or as much as £3,000! The choice you make is important as this will determine if you become a regular detectorist, or just play with the machine for a bit and then put it in the cupboard and forget it. We want you to succeed and enjoy our hobby to the full, so it's better if you get this purchase right first time and avoid wasting your hard-earned money!

We are therefore going to concentrate on the area of the market, which concerns the more basic and cheaper models that the majority of detectorists start out with. However, we are going to ignore the "toys" and will look at serious machines that should serve you well for some time, and find things too!

We are writing and testing the machines in April 2012. We wanted to check different makes of machines that newcomers to the hobby could buy with a certainty that they were suitable and affordable.

Taking only one machine from each manufacturer, we could only come up with a few in the £200 maximum price range. So we have added some second-hand machines, under £200 to the list that are available and selling this month on websites and in *Treasure Hunting* magazine.

There are many places that a detector can be bought. To look at a few:-

- Brand new, or second hand from a dealer in the UK
- Brand new directly from the manufacturer
- Second hand from an advert in *Treasure Hunting* magazine
- From one of the web auctions such as e-Bay
- A car boot sale
- A person down the pub
- Some large stores that sell lesser known makes

Just a word of warning. From time to time machines are stolen from dealers and will find their way onto the open market. So if you are offered a brand new machine from an individual who you don't know, and for a price way below what you might expect, then be wary that you are not about to receive stolen goods!

A SHADY DEAL?

In this chapter is a list of a few detectors that we have chosen from the vast array on offer. In our view all of these seem suitable for anyone new to the hobby; but the list is not complete and we are not saying that other detectors wouldn't be just as suitable. We just had to make a limited selection amongst those that were available to us! We have tried to include some of the more well-known "starter" machines that you will see advertised although any list is, sadly, out of date as soon as a new machine is released by the manufacturer.

A decent new starter detector should cost between £120 and £200. This might seem a bit high, but with the technology that is incorporated in these modern machines, and the quite high resale value, we think this is good value for the money when you are beginning. We have also put in a couple of second hand machines, which are available at the moment for about £200.

If you would like a slightly cheaper option then possibly a second hand detector might be better value. I have bought three second hand machines over the years and normally, as long as a machine looks in good nick and it is working fine when you buy it, you don't seem to get much trouble later on. I have found over the years that detectors seem to go on for ever - I still have two quite old ones that still work very well!

The criteria we have used to look at these models are:-

1. Reasonable cost
2. Easy to assemble
3. Easy to use
4. Ability to find target items on test
5. Quality of pinpointing
6. Weight

Testing the Detectors

Normally, when you read about test results of machines (in magazines, for example) the tester takes them out on to one of his fields and sees what they can find. This is a good working test, but every day is different and every field is different; also, how you detect each day can affect the results. So, in contrast, we decided to be a little more systematic with our testing. We laid out three test beds in grass with each machine only tested against these. This was to ensure that the benchmark was always the same and results would be as fair as possible.

The test bed was laid down over six months before the test, so the ground was as near as possible to the conditions you will find in a field (albeit with the grass being a little shorter, due to my mower, than you normally will encounter on a farm!) Each line of buried objects was then marked out with white tape.

Test bed in my garden.

The tests were:-

1. Six typical "finds", all at a depth of 6 inches
2. Eight "finds" increasing in depth from 2-9 inches
3. Eight identical aluminium tokens increasing in depth from 2-9 inches

Each of us tested each machine independently, and we then averaged our findings. Each machine was used in accordance with the manufacturer's instructions and no attempt was made to adjust the settings more than necessary. Our reason for this was that this is what you would expect to do as somebody new to the hobby.

For the first test we included a couple of coins of different sizes, a lead weight, a small buckle, a button, and a thimble. All of these common test items might be in the finds bag of the average metal detectorist; and at the depth range for any particular object where

The buried items used as targets.

you might expect to find it with a reasonably-priced starter detector.

The prices quoted were about average across the retailers. You will find higher and probably lower; it depends where you shop, and the offers that are on at the time.

We intended to check basic machines. For this we are indebted to Mark and Luke of Joan Allens at Biggin Hill for allowing us to borrow some of the machines with no financial incentive at all.

Detectors Tested

We were pleasantly surprised at the results obtained, as both of us were used to handling more advanced detectors. On the whole, these basic models gave quite good performances in the tests we put them through.

In alphabetical order, here is the list of the detectors that we looked at:-

- Bounty Hunter Tracker 4
- C.Scope CS1MX
- Fisher F2
- Garrett Ace 150
- Minelab X-Terra 305
- Tesoro Laser B1
- Viking 30
- Yellow Joan Allen detector

Before we include any comments, please bear in mind that this is the personal opinion of the two of us; other experienced detectorists might well disagree. We have not received any inducements from manufacturers to favour their machines. We put all the machines through their paces and, in the end, came out with three "best" machines. This rather surprised us as they seemed to be clear of the competition! During testing we were bearing in mind that beginners would not know a lot about how to ultimately "fine tune" detectors; we therefore avoided doing so. The results are listed below, in no particular order.

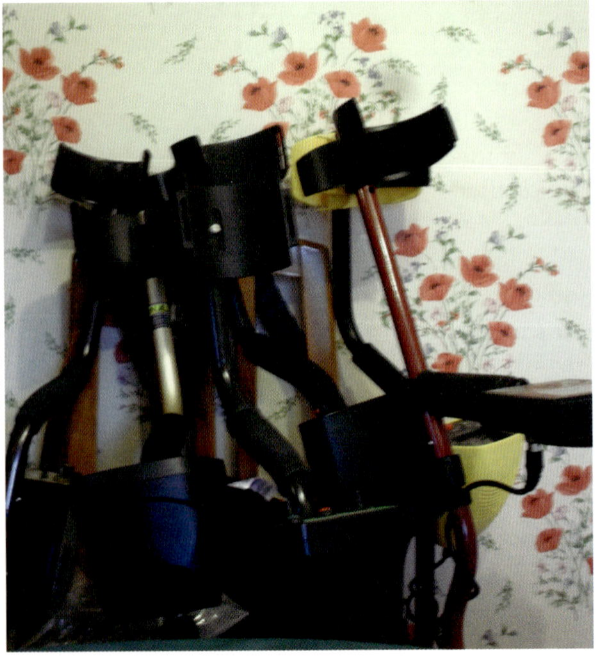

Some of the "starter" detectors we used in the test.

The Minelab X-Terra 305 is a good-looking machine with maroon trim, and is powered by four AA batteries. It is more expensive than the others, but we included it as it is Minilab's "entry" machine. You could find this, second hand, at about £200; it performed reasonably, but not exceptionally. Surprisingly, for two experienced Minelab users, we did not find the controls intuitive.
Points scored - 6 out of 10

The Tracker 4 runs on two PP3 batteries and comes in Bounty Hunter's distinct shape. You can find this model in most dealers for about £145. It is a decent performer, but no more.
Points scored - 6 out of 10

C.Scope were pleased to send us their **CS1MX** by return of post. It is the most basic of their machines, and looks it; but it is very easy to use. It is a motion detector, which means you have to pinpoint the target while keeping the head moving, but this was not a problem. It's powered by one PP3 battery. This was an excellent starter machine, both lightweight and effective at picking up signals. I personally would be very happy to recommend it to anybody.
Points scored - 9 out of 10

The Fisher F2 is both good looking and well laid-out, with gold and black trim. It runs on two PP3 batteries. We liked this one a lot and we felt it performed well above its price range.
Points scored - 9 out of 10

The Garrett Ace 150 despite its bright yellow colour looks and feels like all the higher end Garrett brand models. This one has no pinpoint mode, but the Ace 250, which is slightly dearer, does have this facility. However, it is light and very simple to master, with a beautifully intuitive display. This is another excellent starter machine, particularly for its low price.
Points scored - 8 out of 10

The Viking 30 is a basic looking machine, in green and black trim and powered by one PP3 battery. It is simple to operate, and did reasonably well in the tests, but it is heavy on the arm and rather cumbersome to use. This is a British company and we both really wanted it to do well – sadly it was a disappointment, although we know that dedicated users might disagree.
Points scored - 5 out of 10

The Tesoro Laser B1 is a classic machine that stills produces the goods; the control box is hung underneath the hand grip unlike most modern machines where it's on top. The underneath positioning doesn't matter as there no display to look at anyway. This machine might not have the most up-to-date technology in it, but it showed what it could do in the harder tests. There was one being sold at the time of testing second hand at £150, and it makes the point that you don't have to buy a new machine to start the hobby.
Points scored - 8 out of 10

The prototype **bright yellow box** is a very basic-looking machine that will soon have the **Joan Allen** name on. It's from China, and it's powered up by two PP3 batteries. It did quite well, finding as much as the others and in some cases a bit more. It has a rather old fashioned display needle that seemed a bit erratic, but we are told that this might not be used in the final version.
Points scored - 6 out of 10

NOT A GOOD TEST

Starter Detectors On Test

Conclusions

So what did we find? Any metal detector can spot an old penny on your lounge floor, but not all can find it if it's 6 inches down. Some of the detectors tested missed targets 4 inches down but gave a good signal on another item 6 inches down (i.e. it might miss a button or thimble but find a deeper buckle; this is all to do with shape and metal content, and coil configuration, frequency etc. of the detectors tested). The major manufacture's models, which we have listed, did well enough as starter models.

If, in your wisdom, you do decide to bypass all the starter models, then get some advice from a good dealer - if possible in the shop. Try out a few different types, and compare how they handle. Most dealers want the repeat business of when you upgrade, and the word of mouth recommendations. But, to be honest, some of the machines we tested are so good, and so simple to get going with, then why would you want to buy anything else?

So think about:-

1. Get advice from somebody experienced in the hobby
2. The weight of the machine. This is important after a couple of hours in the field!
3. Is the detector easy or complicated to use?
4. Pinpointing - does it work at depth?
5. The total cost of your new detector. Are headphones, coil cover, and rechargeable batteries included in the package?

Organisations, Clubs and Dealers

After you have bought a metal detector, or even before, you are going to have to decide how you are going to carry on with the hobby. Are you going to detect alone or would you prefer a partner? Would you like to join a nearby club? The one thing you do need is insurance for civil liability cover; this is not for your house, car or dog, and it will not cover you if the river floods and your garden is turned into a lake! No, this is insurance to cover you when you are detecting, just in case somebody sues you because you left a gate open and the escaping cows caused an accident; or a horse broke its leg, because you left an open hole, and ended up being shot. The cost of membership is only, at the time of writing, £6 a year and can be arranged, at your convenience, through the NCMD (for UK residents) via your club membership. The insurance cover is thrown in and is a whopping £10,000,000!

The National Council For Metal Detecting (NCMD)

I have always thought highly of the NCMD, and what it does for detectorists. I believe it provides good value for what you pay as, apart from the insurance, you receive the full back up of their expertise, and experience. The NCMD is the official "voice" of metal detecting. They represent the hobby and argue its point of view with museums and governments alike. Each member of the National Council has been voted on by the regions that cover the whole country, and each of these nine regions is made up of clubs in any one area. The clubs themselves are made up of like-minded people who come together to talk and show their own finds.

NCMD
NATIONAL COUNCIL FOR METAL DETECTING
TO PROMOTE
TO PROTECT
TO ENCOURAGE

The regions are run by representatives of local clubs. Each region runs itself and elects its own committee, and two of these become their region's representatives on the national council. Some regions are better than others for organising events for their members, but these could include display days at museums, farming events, or even days out detecting.

The NCMD has worked hard, since the late 1970s, to ensure that we can legally continue detecting. It regularly meets with Members of Parliament, and helped shape the legislation that brought in the PAS, and the 1996 Treasure Act. So do you need to join a club to get all these benefits? No, you don't, but in my opinion you get more value for your money if you do.

Metal Detecting Clubs

Detecting can be quite a solitary experience. I therefore think that there is nothing better than going to a club meeting where you get to talk to people about what they have found lately, and to be able to show your finds to others. You can also use these meetings to have your finds identified, and recorded on the national finds database run by the PAS. You will also pick up tips from other detectorists.

The FLOs who attend some meetings can also advise finders about an item that might be Treasure under the Act. At our club (Trowbridge MDC) the meetings are always well attended, and very lively. We run competitions for the best coins and artefacts found each month, which encourages people to show and enter their finds. This is where you learn about objects and get to handle things that you might otherwise never see outside of a museum. Photos are taken for our website www.trowbridgemdc.co.uk which then allows anybody to see what has been found; many clubs do something similar and there are some great websites out there for you to explore.

One of the other main benefits for newcomers is that most clubs have access to farmland ("club land"), which means that you always have somewhere to go. Clubs will often arrange days out for members, evening talks or displays of finds for the general public. Some clubs will also own a selection of reference books or equipment that can be lent out to members. Naturally, the quality of a club depends on the drive of its members and that is bound to vary. Popular clubs may well have a waiting list for full membership but still allow you to come to meetings as a guest. You will find them friendly places where experienced detectorists are always happy to help those new to the game.

The Trowbridge Club recently arranged, with the Wiltshire Heritage Museum in Devizes, for a six month long display of

Trowbridge Club's banner.

objects which had been found and recorded by club members. We even had a "launch" one evening with wine and refreshments! We all had a great time and got a buzz out of seeing our finds on public display. This was a whole gallery full of metal detecting finds in six display cases, with over 200 items - and that's not counting the 500 bits of rubbish I collected last year!

So, being in a club can give you contacts and opportunities to really make the most of your new hobby! This Wiltshire Museum is bang up to date (well, the Bronze Age wasn't that long ago) and is well run with some fantastic presentations. It's in an old building with a maze of rooms where the upstairs floors creak, but that's all part of its charm. There is a lift for those who need it, and it's a very child-friendly place. You will find it in Long Street, just five minutes away from the market place or the Station car park (but no Station) where there is plenty of parking in both. This would make a good day out for the children, while you brush up on your knowledge and see some of the many fantastic items which you could be finding while out detecting.

Small part of the museum display.

You will find their Web site at http://www.wiltshireheritage.org.uk/

Not A Club Person?

You don't have to belong to a club to get the benefits of the NCMD. They realised that not everybody wants to socialise with other detectorists. You can be completely independent and still have the backup of the National Council. To do this, all you have to do is join as an independent member from the website www.ncmd.co.uk

and you will then get the full colour magazine *Digging Deep*; the insurance described above, for when you are out detecting; and the same full support that club members get via their clubs. This will cost you annually £8 (current April 2012).

Dealers & Stockists

There are many dealers in this country who stock and sell metal detectors; you can find adverts in *Treasure Hunting* magazine, and also on the web. We've tried to include a complete list at the back of this book (apologies if we left anyone out). Dealers are normally very helpful when you are buying a detector and, if you can, visit the shop in person as you can see and handle the machines and get expert advice on the model that will suit you (and your pocket!). For more complex machines you can also get help on setting a programme. This is also one of the advantages of joining a club where, perhaps, you can try another member's particular machine before you order one yourself. Dealers will also sell all the accessories you might want ranging from pinpoint probes to books, and diggers to batteries.

Manufacturers

Metal detectors are made in the UK, America, Germany, and many other countries. As a rule of thumb, I would recommend that you buy a detector (wherever its country of origin) from a dealer in the UK. You could hit problems if you buy a machine that has been imported privately and does not have warranty or repair back-up.

There is such a good selection of well-known manufacturers that there is no real need to buy from a non-reputable source, and I list the more obvious firms, and their contact details, at the back of the book. Be very wary about amazing offers on unusual machines quoted in newspapers or anywhere else. Stick to well-known machines bought from recognised dealers, direct from the manufacturer or from individuals whom you trust. Remember the maxim: if it seems too good to be true, it probably is!

Where To Search and Ten Ways To Gain Permission

IT'S STILL POSSIBLE

So you have all the equipment you need, insurance from the NCMD, and a detector that has all the technology to send a spacecraft to the moon. But you still have nowhere to go! So what do you do now? This is the hardest part when starting the hobby and it's also the easiest when you know how; and that is what we are going to show you. So let's remember what the law, and our Code of Practice, says: "You must have permission to detect on virtually any land in this country." All land is owned by, or is managed by, somebody. So you have to find a way of getting permission to search it.

First a word of caution! Ladies, you need to be extra cautious when trying to gain permission. I always advise our lady members never to detect on their own, and to always let somebody else know they are going, and when they can expect you to return. Nowadays a fully charged mobile phone is also a must - for all detectorists.

So let's look at where, in theory, it's possible to detect, and how to go about getting permission. So how can you get permission to detect?

How do you find somebody who will allow you, a complete stranger, to come and go when you like, to walk across their land, disturb their animals, dig holes, pocket anything you find, and disappear? It's like you inviting a stranger to come into your garden, whenever they like, make themselves at home, and dig up your flower beds. But it can be done and this is how!

Where To Search and Ten Ways To Gain Permission

Let's leave it at 10 (yes, 10!) ways to get permission, as they seem the most obvious. When you look through this list the one thing that jumps out at you is how each sentence starts: "You can". They are two very small words but by remembering them you have nearly cracked it. You can get permission if you make an effort; there is always a reason for not having enough land to detect on throughout the year. That reason is you, for if you want land you have to work at it. Some people just seem to have the knack, or are very lucky, but most of us find it a little more difficult.

When writing to anybody, a stamped address envelope is essential if you want them to reply. Without this, your letter could very well end up in the bin.

Whatever method you use, you have to give the farmer an honest statement of how you mean to conduct yourself, by keeping him informed about what you find, and that you have to obey the law in respect of the 1996 Treasure Act. We would strongly encourage you to use the Portable Antiquities Scheme to report your normal finds, but you need to explain this to the farmer as a few might get a little suspicious about it. So let's look at farmland first, as it tends to make up the majority of land that we detect on.

Method 1: You can write a letter to a named farmer

If you use this method you have to keep it short and to the point, and always include the essentials: what you want to do; where you would like to detect; when is it okay; that you are fully insured; and that holes will be small and well filled in. With all letters you have to remember that farmers are busy people and receive a lot of rubbish through the post. So your letter must not be long winded, but rather convey a short interesting message to him.

PERMISSION OR NOT?

Method 2: You can write a standard letter and send it to lots of farms in any one area

The standard letter is really a copy of the first letter, but it should

52 Roman Hoard Rd
Frome
Somerset
54A D20
Tel: 52503 52503
Potfull@Roma.co.uk

10 April 2010

Dear Mr. Smith,

My name is Dave Crisp, and I am writing to see if I can ask you for permission to come metal detecting on your land. I am fully insured with third party civil liability cover; no damage is done by my detecting, and holes are always small and well filled in.

I do not detect on growing crops, and I always observe the Countryside Code.

I am a member of the National Council of Metal Detecting, which is recognised by the National Farmers Union, and I am also completely aware of the law on reporting items that could be Treasure. Of course, I would show you anything that I find that is interesting first.

I would like to come and see you to talk about this, at your convenience. I have enclosed a stamped addressed envelope with my phone number and e-mail address, if you would rather contact me that way.

Thank you for reading and considering this request.

Yours Sincerely

Mr. D. Crisp

be personalised by naming the farmer rather than "Dear Sir", and also by signing it personally. This also calls for a self-addressed envelope, but now the costs go up! A sample letter is included above.

Method 3: You can visit a farmer after phoning and getting an appointment

Farmers work seven days a week, and are always busy, so to get an appointment you have to be brief, interesting, and persuasive. Before you phone make a small list of what you really need to say. This call is "make or break". If you get an interview you have normally cracked it. Be on time and keep it as short as possible; cover all the points, and don't waffle. Let them tell you what they want out of this; it could be just information about what you find on their farm, or they might want some of the things you find. Farmers are all different.

Method 4: You can cold call (i.e. just visit a farm and hope there's somebody there)

This is a hit or miss way of doing things, but it does work if you are persistent and miss the farmer the first time. I have always found that by seeing his wife, or somebody who works on the farm in advance, you get a feel for how your meeting will go. As with all meetings be prepared, know what you are going to say, and have a short list of points you want to get over. The two points I always stress when talking, or writing, to farmers are that I am fully insured, and that no holes or mess will be left.

Method 5: You can take out an advert in the local paper

Placing an advertisement in the local paper might not cost too much, but you have to accept that you might not get any replies or, even worse, replies from the wrong people (there are some funny people out there!).

Method 6: You can advertise on web sites

This is a modern version of Method 5, but allows you to say more for no extra cost. The downside is that you need to find a website that farmers regularly read, and you have to catch their eye; but some web sites will allow your message to stay on as long as you wish.

Method 7: You can put an advert in one of the farming magazines

This is a direct method of getting your message across to a large number of the type of people that you wish to ask, but this does not mean that you will get more, or even any, replies. The other disadvantage is the large geographical area that you will be targeting, so if you are only going to be detecting in, say a 20 mile radius, you could get your only reply from 50 miles away.

Method 8: You can sit in a local pub and hope a farmer comes in, and then buy him a drink!

It is probably one of the most enjoyable methods, but is very hit or miss, and more miss then hit as the night goes on. Hic! But just making friends in a country pub has its compensations!

BUY HIM A PINT

Method 9: You can get an introduction from a friend, who knows a farmer/ landowner/farm worker/ contractor/a chicken

Quite a good method, as long as you don't live in the middle of London or Birmingham. If you live in a smallish place close to farmland the chances are you know somebody, or that person knows somebody, who knows a farmer, or it might be somebody who works on a farm, or gets fresh eggs or shops at a farm shop.

PERHAPS THE CHICKEN KNOWS

Method 10: You can stop and talk to a farm worker, as you are driving by

This method is quite a good one, but you need to be willing to talk to a complete stranger in the middle of nowhere, and at the same time you have to be able to get your questions across. This is not always such a good way, as you have to be able park your car quickly and sensibly in a fairly convenient place, and be a confident talker. You might also need to drive around country lanes a lot in the hope of seeing somebody just standing there.

You should be aware that not everybody standing in a gate way works on a farm, so this way should be used with caution!

So we have 10 different ways of talking to farmers, but none of these will guarantee you get what you want, and that is permission to detect on some land. "Why not?" you say! Farmers are the salt of the earth; they are also very hardworking people, educated, and down to earth - sometimes miserable, sometimes happy - just like you and me. They too have good and bad days. So every time is different and remember, it is their land and they simply might just not want anybody there.

MAYBE SHE'S A FARMER

Where To Search and Ten Ways To Gain Permission

Be polite, ask nicely, do not argue, and be prepared to thank them and walk away.

Tenant Farmers

Not all land is owned by the person farming it; if it is rented then you have to have permission from both the landowner and the tenant. This is one where a written agreement could be worthwhile (see "Written Agreements" later on).

Councils

Some farmland is owned by councils, along with parkland and, perhaps, the village green, so it's a case of writing to explain what you would like and to ask how you should go about it. Councils, land agents, committees etc. all have policies that cover all aspects of how they operate and this will include who can do what on their land. This is what you have to get past. First you have to find out who owns the piece of land, then who manages it, where they are, who you have to speak to, and how to contact them. In this case a phone call into the maze of a local, or district, council office can help to narrow down who is responsible for the administration of the land you are interested in.

The key here is not taking the first person's word that you cannot. Politely insist that you are going to write, asking for permission, and that you expect a written reply stating why permission is not being granted.

If you encounter problems you could always speak to your local councillor (their names are normally in the phone book), to find out if they know of any rules, bye laws etc. Remember you are a council tax payer! But don't just steam in, you might need somebody on your side!

As with letters to farmers, you have to keep your request as short as possible, but get your point across. Ensure that you cover all the main points:-

- Fully Insured
- No holes and mess
- No damage, no gates left open
- Knowledge of the Treasure Act
- Reporting possible Treasure
- Member of the NCMD

Local Common Land (you know the type of thing - the bit in the middle called the village green, or if it's in the town it's called "the common"), is normally run by a local or district council. The Countryside and Rights of Way Act 2000 increased access to common land (referred to as "access land" in the Act) and gave people more extensive rights; but this does not mean you can detect on it. If you do get permission, get it in writing, and carry it with you because, as sure as eggs are eggs, somebody will complain when you are there!

SOME PLACES DON'T BOTHER

Consecrated ground, such as churchyards, is to be avoided; you're not going to gain permission and it is just a little morbid. A lady did once ask me once if I thought she could get permission to detect in a churchyard; I let her down gently. For non-consecrated church ground the Diocese in your area, that runs churches and church land, would have to be the first port of call.

Mountains, Moors & Hills

If it's not private land then it's part of an estate belonging to the council, Crown Estate, National Trust, Forestry Commission, and so is somewhere, somebody's responsibility to oversee it. Here is where local knowledge comes in. A phone call here or a visit to a local house can pay dividends, to ascertain who owns, or runs a particular piece of land. MOD land is usually out of bounds, although you are welcome to try and get permission if you can!

Canal Paths are owned and run by British Waterways, and they do not allow detecting. In the last few years plenty of tow paths have been renovated which has meant the original surface being covered with a good layer of chippings, gravel or hardcore - none of which would help detecting! But as you are not allowed to detect on them, it doesn't really matter.

Where To Search and Ten Ways To Gain Permission

Beach Permission

Beaches are like Marmite, you love them or you hate them. But in my view there is no point of going to one without a detector. It is where people have been scattering their belongings for the last 2000 years. It's just like a field that has been well used on a daily basis; but fields just don't get washed twice a day.

There is nothing better than going to a nice beach on a summer's day, getting some sun, reading a good book, maybe a swim in the ocean, a bite of lunch and perhaps a little snooze. Then, when other people are packing up and the beach is going quiet, getting out the detector for the real reason for being there. Modern losses are always going to be your main finds, but there is always a chance of earlier lost items. Remember that all valuable finds should be reported, but going into the local police station with a couple of quid's worth of loose change, is not going to go down well. Buy yourself an ice cream! I know somebody who found a £20 note presumably rolled up for sniffing (seaweed?). It was just being blown along on top of the sand. Keep your eyes on the surface of the beach - you never know.

The majority of our beaches in this country are run by the local council, where blanket permission is granted, alongside all the other activities. But there are a few exceptions to this rule.

The National Trust (sadly) doesn't allow detecting on their beaches, and private beaches seem not to allow it either (although you can always ask!). The Crown Estate also runs some stretches of foreshore and they have a scheme where you can get a permit to detect down to the low water mark. You will find their web address in the address section at the back. Here you can check their maps, and download a permit.

ONE EYE ON THE TIDE

There are specialised (and expensive) metal detectors that are fully waterproofed and are used by undersea archaeologists or "treasure hunters", but it is probably a little hard to swim and detect at the same time and most normal detectors work perfectly well with the head submerged.

Flotsam, Jetsam & Lagan

You should also be aware of items that you might find on the beach that have been washed in, and what you should do if you find anything. Basically there are flotsam, jetsam and lagan.

"Jetsam" refers to any goods that were deliberately thrown off a ship in danger, to save itself. "Flotsam" is goods that floated off the ship, by chance, while it was in danger or when it sank. "Lagan" is goods left in the sea on the wreck or tied to a buoy so that they can be recovered later by the owners. This will all be very handy to know in a pub quiz, so pay attention.

If you find something valuable that has been washed up on the beach, however small, you should report it to the "Receiver of Wreck". There are hefty fines for not reporting something that is wreck.

The Receiver will investigate the ownership of the item, normally while you hold on to it. This could include gold coins, bells and fixtures from a ship. After a year, if they cannot find the owner, it becomes property of the Crown, and the Receiver can dispose of it and, often, the finder is allowed to keep the unclaimed wreck in lieu of a reward. You should also be aware that there are items washed up that are dangerous (e.g. mines, flares, chemicals drums etc.). The current Receiver is Alison Kentuck and the present contact details are in the back of this book along with a copy of the reporting form you should use.

In London there is a scheme that allows metal detecting on the Thames Foreshore but you need a licence from the Port of London Authority and on some sections have to belong to the Society of Mudlarks. This is probably one of the most dangerous places to detect if you don't know what you are doing. When the tide turns, the mud you are standing on can be covered in water very fast, and you can be easily cut off!

Are Detectorist/Landowner Agreements Worthwhile?

So you caught Mr. Farmer in a good mood and he has listened to what you have said and then agreed you can detect. "Just help yourself!" he said, and waved you off.

- Should you have some sort of agreement?
- Should it be verbal (as it is now) or be written down?
- Is it worth it?
- Will he be offended if you ask?
- What if he says no?
- What happens if you find something good?
- What happens if you find a hoard of Roman coins? (I did)
- Will he deny giving permission?

What does the law say? The consensus is that it is better to get permission in writing. But every time you get permission it's different; it's a different farmer, and different land, so you have to make up your mind at the time or come back and bring up the subject. Presumably you have already talked about the points mentioned earlier, and he has marked your map to show where you can go. Now comes the tricky bit: ask if he would like a written agreement showing who you are, where you live, and what would happen to any finds that you might make. He might welcome it, or he might just say no, or ask why. Here you have to be a bit of a diplomat and mention again about the Treasure Act and the reporting of items that fall under it.

You do not need a written agreement and, although it has its advantages, I have never had one and, up to today, I have never had any trouble. But I always make it clear how we stand. I do all my agreeing face to face, and I always send them a letter thanking them for permission, and restating all the points that we have discussed.

A copy of the NCMD and National Farmers Union written agreement is printed at the end of the book. This can be used as a base agreement, and altered to suite yourself.

"I am a great fan of the Portable Antiquities Scheme. It has a tremendous ability to engage all sorts of people with an interest in archaeology, including those who find objects and those who want to learn about them. I'd like to pay tribute to every one involved with the scheme, especially its finds liaison officers and the many people who have promptly and properly reported their finds. Thanks to them we can all experience something of the thrill of discovery and learn more about the past."

Ed Vaizey Culture Minister 2011

Scheduled Land

This is land that has been marked by the government to legally protect and conserve it. These sites are designated by the Secretary of State and this means you cannot detect on them. Even archaeologists have to get written permission to do digs of any sort. How do you know if it is scheduled? Well, you have to find out. Some places are obvious, like Stonehenge, but some are only marked on maps, if at all. Some libraries will hold a copy of a list, but it's not necessarily up to date. Your Finds Liaison Officer might be able to help and, of course, the farmer or landowner should know; but remember they cannot give you permission to go on that land. If you do find a Scheduled Monument then walk away; there's plenty of other land out there.

So there you have it. You can get permission, but not always for your first choice land, and it's not always easy. But there is plenty of land available, and if you do get refused, don't argue and don't curse if you are sure it's a "No". Just politely thank them for their time and walk away. If it's a council type of refusal, and it is policy, then it's probably written in stone and you will not have much chance of changing it. If it's a vague "No", and nobody can tell you where it's written down, then challenge it. You never know what you can do till you try, so good luck! But remember, it's up to you!

Farmers & Landowners

They come in all shapes and sizes, good, bad and indifferent. They can be very helpful, indifferent or downright stubborn with you, but in the end you need their cooperation and trust if you want to detect on their land, or even to get past the front door. They are normally down to earth, practical, helpful, and sometimes even interested, but they are always busy.

Neil and a few of his cows.

This is one of the good farmers, Neil, with some of his Montbeliardes milking cows. Note he's happy, and that these Montbeliardes cows look different from the Friesian shown in the next chapter. Neil's cows are bred for high quality milk and with heifers and male calves matured for high quality beef. (Roast beef served slightly pink, with Yorkshires. Mm, sounds good) Sorry, I digress.

The fact is farmers are just like you and me; they have good days and bad days; some are the salt of the earth, and some should be under it. So, when you get permission, respect their wishes, their land, the crops, and their animals. Take every opportunity to talk to them and their family members. Always remember the kids: I am still detecting on farms, now farmed by the kids I met there 20 years ago.

Always show your finds if they seem interested; some are very interested, and some don't want to know. Some will believe you won't find anything; show them that there is always something of interest. Get a copy of your PAS sheets and make up a folder of the farm finds for them. If they seem to really like an item, be generous and let them have it. Think about making up a small box of selected and labelled items and present it to them. It will pay dividends in the long run. Always remember we have this hobby only because of their generosity.

Also, remember that if you have the permission of a tenant farmer, then you also need the permission of the landowner. It can cause a lot of problems later otherwise.

It's a nice gesture if at Christmas you gave your farmer a bottle or two, even if you haven't found anything, and a Christmas card wouldn't go amiss. (Make sure they know who it's from.)

FARMERS - SALT OF THE EARTH

The Dangers of the Farm

KEEP AN EYE OUT FOR ANIMALS

One of the funniest things I have ever seen, a few years ago, was a member of our club being slowly chased across a field by a fat cow who obviously only wanted to be milked. The poor thing had been forgotten in the field and wanted to get back into the milking parlour. The cow was old and full of milk, and could not run, but it could bellow and the more it bellowed the faster my mate ran.

However, that story has a serious side to it. Farms are one of the most dangerous places to work and so, by definition, can also be hazardous for us. Whether driving, parking, walking, or detecting, you have to take reasonable precautions. But by using the knowledge you will have gained in this chapter, and a bit of common sense, you can metal detect in relative safety.

Driving & Parking

The first point is when you are driving up the lane or track to the farm; you may encounter tractors, diggers, or Land Rovers pulling overflowing trailers with loads that would not be legal on public roads. Combine harvesters are probably the widest things you will meet, so are better given a wide berth. The same applies to the muck spreaders, but for different reasons. At least it makes the roses grow!

These vehicles are using the same track as you and sod's law says they will be going in the opposite direction. Dave's (first) Law says: "Give way to them, it's easier".

Some of farm tracks are well paved and some are surfaced with tarmac. But others are like driving through a war zone, and you have to have all your wits about you. Look out for ruts, cow pats, and pot holes (big enough to swallow a small car), to say nothing of farm animals, children and a variety of domestic fowl such as chickens, ducks, geese, guinea fowl, pheasants, partridge and, potentially, even ostriches! And that's even before you park.

Don't overestimate the ability of your family two-wheel drive saloon. Farmers have better things to do than tow you out of a ditch! If in doubt, walk!

Where you actually park should have been agreed at your meeting with the farmer when you obtained permission; but you should always park in such a way that you are not blocking gates, drives, trackways, entrances to barns etc. So the most convenient for you near the fields, is not necessary the best place for the farmer. On a working farm, you will encounter tractors, trailers, combines, forklifts, or 4x4s all working in a tight area, which could involve turning or backing. So a badly parked car could hamper their work and endanger yourself and your car. There are nearly always places to park out of the way, and if you park there, then you are more likely not to be involved in any incident or accident.

Should I Detect Alone?

However you choose to go detecting, you have to think about safety, particularly if you are female. Obviously if you go detecting with a partner or a few members of your club, you can keep an eye on one another. It's also good to have a companion so you can compare finds, and when you get the unidentifiable or a fantastic item it's great to have somebody to show it to. But if you do go alone then take a mobile phone and ensure that you know the details of the farm. It's a sensible idea to have the farmer's mobile number (they are rarely at home) stored in your phone. This could be handy if you twist an ankle or discover the hoard of the century (it happens!). A normal size farm can have a dozen or more fields, and the majority of the time you could be well out of sight of anybody.

Rats & Ticks

A tick is a very small bug that lives on cows, pigs, horses, deer and a lot of the smaller animals. During their life cycle they drop off into the grass to change hosts. This is where they climb up the stems of grass, stalks of crops or small bushes to wait for another animal to come along. They then attach themselves to the skin or hide of that new host where they burrow into the flesh. Being intelligent creatures they especially target metal detectorists as we walk through vegetation and where they can reach the skin of ankles and legs. They then proceed to suck blood and in so doing can transfer the bacteria which can cause Lyme's disease. A rash can form, where you have been bitten, with a white ring. This is quite distinctive and can be particularly nasty. It can cause swelling of the legs, pain in the joints and muscles, with dizziness and palpitations and sensitivity to light. It is better if the ticks are removed early, but they are sometimes hard to see due to their small size. If found they should be removed with a pair of tweezers, taking care not to crush the body or its head. If in doubt, see your GP and think twice before detecting in shorts!

A nasty looking tick, which could be a different colour and about 5-6mm.

Rats, which live in the countryside, can pass on Weill's disease from their urine which can then survive in the water of puddles through which you walk. This is a good reason to wash or disinfect your hands before eating your lunch. I carry, in my lunch pack, a small bottle of hand disinfectant gel just for this purpose. The bacteria responsible for this problem can enter through a cut or wet hands if you were to wipe your mouth or get splashed from a puddle. The symptoms can be mild, but a fever is often apparent for 3 to 15 days. Throughout this period muscle pains, headaches, tiredness and aversion to bright lights, hallucinations, sore throat and a dry cough could also be present. Again, if you are unsure then seek medical advice.

Having scared you all, both of these diseases are quite rare in this country, and I personally have never heard of a metal detectorist contacting either!

Aren't Tractors Big!

When on farm land, or any other land, you should always be aware of your surroundings. Even with your headphones on, you must be able to hear any tractors, or any other farm vehicles, approaching which just might not see you if they are concentrating on what they are doing! Always give a cheery wave to the driver as he might stop and chat; also, before you know it, you might have information that might lead to permission on another farm! Just walking across a grass field has a proportion of danger if you were to put your foot into a hole and twist your ankle - and that has often happened. A freshly ploughed field can have ruts a foot deep, with soft or wet soil hiding a multitude of dangers. Therefore walking over these can be treacherous.

Cows Are Big Too!

There are instances of people having been killed by cows, and these animals can be very dangerous. Cows are funny creatures to look at from the other side of the gate of the field they are in, but that can be deceptive.

Young heifers can be very inquisitive - to the point of being a significant problem if you go into their field. Youngsters will always come and investigate you and it's their curiosity that can lead to those at the back pushing forwards, and those at the front trying to back away. It's at this point that they start to get excited and to turn, kick, and butt.

Young Friesian cows being nosy.

Older cows are more docile, and normally okay when you are crossing their field; but they can be unpredictable. Cows may also think you are coming to feed them and, if feeling peckish can run towards you en masse. They will mean you no harm, but if you're not used to this it can be very scary and potentially dangerous.

So, what do you do? Remember cows are not normally aggressive so to fend them off just stand your ground, wave your arms about, and make a lot of noise. That should do the trick. Never, when attempting this, hem them in. Always give them an escape route so they can run away. When it's all calmed down – go to another field! I personally never try searching a field full of livestock, there are plenty more fields they are not in.

Bulls Are Bigger Still!

They say that if you grab a bull by the ring through its nose you can lead him anywhere. I would say that whoever said that had a death wish! Stay away from a bull; keep him in sight if you're crossing a field, and don't get in between him and his cows. He can run very fast, but how fast can you run? I don't believe that farmers would put a dangerous animal in a field with a footpath crossing it intentionally, but does the bull know that?

Dave's (second) Law: if you don't have to go in that particular field, why bother?

Horses

Like cows horses can be inquisitive but unlike bulls are rarely aggressive; on the other hand they are big and fast and can get quite frisky. Many horse owners are uneasy about detectorists going into the same field as their animals so unless you have specific permission, such areas are best avoided.

Sheep

Sheep are fine as they will always back away from you or run like hell. I have never heard about any trouble from a flock of sheep, and they have an added bonus that they taste nice. However, don't go anywhere near them in the lambing season!

Unusual Animals

In the last few years there has been a tendency to have a range of somewhat unusual (if not exotic) animals on some farms. So to name a few you could come in contact with are llamas, alpacas, buffalo, camels, and ostrich: we are really becoming a cosmopolitan farming community.

STRANGE COMPANIONS

Pigs

Pigs on a farm manage to dig up and move any amount of edible and inedible things, one of these items happens to be the field itself. They can manage to change a normal field into something that resembles a war-torn battlefield. Why would any sensible person detect on something like this? I just leave them alone and come back when the field has been returned to normal; what they haven't managed to eat will still be there then.

Children, Pets and Other Animals

There are three types of children on a farm: yours, theirs, and other visitors'. Children don't see danger as we see it; a farm is either a home where they have grown up or a place of enjoyment.

When driving in or out of a farm watch out for kids and, if you take older children with you, make sure you know where they are and what they are doing at all times. In our club we have a few youngsters, which is great as we need young people to be interested just to keep the hobby going. But we emphasise that the parent must be responsible. Don't bring small children with you to a farm – it's just too dangerous. Likewise never bring the dog with you unless the farmer has agreed to this (which he probably won't).

Mushrooms

Do you know your mushroom from your toadstool? Can you tell the difference between a Puffball and a Death Cap? No? Well I can, but I still don't pick fungi in the fields. A few years ago, as a chef, I tasted a wild mushroom risotto that tasted fantastic, but tasting that dish did not make me an expert on the difference between an edible type and one that would lay me low or even kill me. You will come across many varied and different types of fungi when you are walking the fields and woods of this country. If you are an expert on fungi, or have a done a university course in the identification of mushrooms and toadstools then that's fine; otherwise leave them alone, that way you will live to detect another day.

MUSHROOM OR NOT SURE?

The Slurry Pit

This is like a swimming pool, or pond, filled with cow poo, urine and old hay. This, after being fermented to a deep thick lumpy stew, is then spread across the fields to make the plants grow. There are normally warning signs around the pit, but your nose will tell you where it is. Stay well away, it can kill. I don't know why anybody would want to get anywhere near it, but it's not worth the trouble and contains few or no finds!

It may seem that I am labouring all the bad points of a farm, but in with the pleasure you get from detecting you must remember what could happen. With common sense you can enjoy years of detecting without anything bad happening to you or yours.

KEEP OUT OF THE WAY!

Getting Shot

Many farms allow game shooting on their land; some even have organised game shoots at certain times of the year and this can be a valuable source of revenue for the farmer. The main game season for pheasants is from October to the end of January, but rough shooting (e.g. vermin: such as rabbits, grey squirrels and rats) can be going on at any time. Quite often people have permission for this just to keep the rabbit population down. So, although this tends to happen in the early evening, be aware at all times.

You should make yourself aware of any shooting that might be going on in the farm, or in the near vicinity. Ask the farmer for the dates of any organised shoots, and just stay away on those days. If you stumble across a shoot, beat a dignified retreat to your car and, as you do, stay away from hedges - you might not look like a pheasant, but why take a chance? The majority of this type of shooting is with a shotgun, so the shot doesn't travel far, but it can be a bit unnerving to hear a gun going off close to you.

The "season" for game (i.e. when they can be shot), including deer, is different in different parts of the country; but it's more prevalent from 12 August (grouse), round to the end of February (deer). There is some comfort as it is an offence to kill game on a Sunday or Christmas Day. I have always wondered if it's because they can go to church? There are also gun clubs that do clay pigeon shooting where small round composite targets are fired into the air. You tend to get a lot more noise, but they should be shooting upwards. So, unless you are a pigeon, and not too close, you should be safe.

Getting Blown Up

It's very possible that you might dig up some ordnance (ammunition to you and me). The majority of items will be Second World War vintage, like the hand grenade base plug shown, but everything should be viewed with caution. Mortar shells, shell casings or ammunition could still be live even if badly corroded, and should not be handled. If you find something that you believe is dangerous, then you should call the police. They, in turn, after inspecting the item will probably call the Bomb Squad.

A fuse from a Second World War hand grenade.

I found a live mortar shell from the Second World War, back in 2006; when I realised what it was I placed it in the ditch to keep it safe. This was to ensure my farmer didn't drive over it while I called for help. After showing the police where it was, I got told off for digging it up and moving it. (It's a funny old world, how can you find out what something is, without digging it up?)

Lead

Lead has been used throughout the ages for the making of all sorts of items, and it is certain that you will find your share of bits and pieces when out detecting. The Romans, in particular, were great lead workers. The soft metal corrodes easily to form a white coating of lead oxide, and this is toxic. If you have been unearthing lead your hands should always be well washed before eating your lunch, and resist the temptation of giving old musket balls to children.

The Dangers of the Farm

Snakes

We are now scraping the bottom of the barrel of risks, as I have never seen or even heard of anybody seeing a snake when out detecting. But in Great Britain we do have two native types: one is the grass snake which is completely harmless; and the other is the adder, commonly called a viper. The bite of the adder is rarely fatal, but you should always get medical help as soon as possible. Adders are protected under the Wildlife and Countryside Act 1981 and so it is an offence to kill or harm them in any way. (Not that you were going to do so).

Places to Go and Fields to See

Farmers use any number of methods of dividing one field from another. Hedges must be the most common, and then fences, ditches, and walls, which are normally dry stone. Hedges, and dry stone walling also provide a home for plenty of birds and mammals.

The common factor in all these constructions is that of gates, and these are there to be used. You will not be flavour of the month with the farmer if he sees you breaking down his field boundaries. The normal rule on farms is: if it's open then leave it; if it's closed, then close it behind you. In the latter case always ensure they are latched or locked. A barbed wire fence is very tempting to go under or over, until you ruin a good coat, or something more delicate. If a gate is securely locked, and reasonably sturdy, then it should be fine to climb over it...but be sensible!

You might also come across an electric fence consisting of just one or two strands of wire that look very innocent. But why do the animals stay away from them? A few years ago we had a club outing when we encountered one of these fences and I, being a gentleman, held down the top strand with my digger (it had a rubber handle) for two girls to cross. I helped one over, and she held the other girl's hand; however, that girl touched the wire. Watchers said it looked really funny all three of us twitching and jumping. Tony, unlike myself, always carries a magnetic compass in his rucksack. He can tell if the wire is live by looking for a deviation in the compass needle. (I had to look up the word deviation to see if it was legal).

Farm Watch

Finally, when you are out and about on farms, it's worth keeping your eyes open for anything suspicious as there is an increasing amount of rural crime being committed. Farms are being targeted by thieves for equipment and diesel. So if you see anything doubtful then it's worth checking with the farmer, and if that's not possible then a call to Farm Watch, run by the police, might be worthwhile.

Down here in Wiltshire our rural crime team is run by P.C. Bordiss on: 0845 408 7000 ext. 739 817 or 07968942116 or email: ruralcrimeteam@wiltshire.pnn.police.uk

I am sure that all areas of the UK have something similar and you might like to find out your local equivalent. With numbers on your mobile phone of your farmer and your local P.C., at least you can contact somebody and get it checked out. You can also contact crime stoppers on 0800 555 111 or the police non-emergency number 101 .

So if you haven't been kicked by a horse, trampled by heifers, drowned in a slurry pit, poisoned by wild mushrooms, eaten alive by rabbits, or run over by the combine harvester, it must have been a good day's detecting. Stay safe, and have many more.

Detecting Land

In this chapter I am going to look at the type of land you are going to find when you go through that farm gate. You have to remember that these are working farms and the fields, on that particular day, are as they are for a reason. For us, farmland is basically divided into two sorts: arable (growing crops) or pasture (grassland). Farms can be one or the other, or a combination of both, and the mix can change from one year to the next.

HANDY IF THE GRASS IS LONG

From John O' Groats to Land's End, from Bangor to the Wash, different crops are grown, and different farming practices are used. The type of soil, the weather, and current food prices all play a part in a farmer's decision as to how his land should be used.

You need to know exactly when the best time to go to certain farms is, and when you should avoid getting in the farmer's way! It all depends on the crop cycle, and the time of year.

Arable Land

Let's take arable land first, which just means that crops are grown on a regular basis. So each field will change with the seasons, and you will get a wide variety of different land conditions. Arable crops grown in Britain could include barley, wheat, maize, oil seed rape (the bright yellow fields in April/May), potatoes, peas, sugar beet, beans, turnips, swede and, no doubt, many others. In the last few years a few more exotic crops have crept in, such as elephant grass, which is used to power small heating systems on farms (and some is even grown to fuel power stations). Not bad for a crop which is really just grass! Mind you, it does grow 12 feet high and is impregnable to almost everything except birds!

"The high number of finds recorded is testament to the tremendous success of the Portable Antiquities Scheme and the Treasure Act, and I am delighted that we have been able to agree new contracts with all the partners in the Scheme, so the current posts will continue. The finds reported though the Portable Antiquities Scheme and Treasure are changing our understanding of the past, helping archaeologists learn where people lived and died, and how these finds were used. But what is truly exciting, is that these finds are being made by the public not (in most cases) by archaeologists, transforming the archaeological map of Britain."

Neil McGregor, Director of the British Museum

The Arable Year

So we come to what happens on a farm that grows crops during the course of the year. We have to start somewhere, so let's start in January when most of the land is dormant (i.e. nothing is really growing, but some fields could contain a crop that was sown in the previous autumn, such as winter barley). On some of your fields you might have the stubble from last year, as this is left to rot and ploughed back in to help improve the soil's fertility. When the fields are left like this it gives you a whole winter in which to detect and, as the stubble rots and softens, the conditions just get better.

Sometimes the field is ploughed at the end of the year. This allows the weather to break down the farrowed soil, and makes the next job (harrowing) a lot easier. However, this is only normally done if the farmer has the time.

An old stubble field.

When a field is just ploughed and left, it will gradually get better to detect on as the months progress. Some farmers just leave it until about March and this will give you a few more months to detect. Early in the year (March or April) a famer will, as soon as possible, start to prepare his fields by ploughing, dicing, harrowing, and rolling. All this has to be done before he can plant his seeds for the next harvest to grow.

A nice ploughed and rolled field.

Basically he ploughs the field to turn in last year's stubble (what's left after harvesting), and the muck that he has spread over it. This is all the waste products from the cattle, and the extra that he has been keeping in a slurry pit (a mixture of cattle dung and straw bedding from the cattle sheds). This is all sprayed on the land before he ploughs it in. Sometimes the muck will be gradually spread over the winter months. Therefore, if you go out in this, remember to scrape your boots before going home.

He will then use a dicer, which is a very large set of stainless steel blades, to break down the turned earth into smaller pieces. He might then do it all again the other way across the field to break it down even further, or he might use the "ram" or rollers. These are like large heavy rolling pins, dragged behind the tractor to flatten the ground. At this time, depending on what crops he is growing, he might also spread pellets of fertiliser. This is a good time to get some detecting hours in!

Otherwise he will plough, disk harrow, and seed the field all in one go and, from when he starts, you will be amazed at the speed that he can turn stubble into seeded land. All this work has to be done to provide the correct growing environment for the seed to sprout and grow easily. If he is lucky, he will have all of this ready just as the weather is warming up the soil, to help the plants. So when the conditions are right he seeds, and maybe rolls it down flat with the ram to firm the soil.

Now at this point he might allow you to detect, as you really cannot do any harm. However, once the seed starts to sprout you have to check again, as some farmers will allow you to search in such conditions and some, with a vengeance, will not. At this time of the year the conditions are perfect for detecting as the land has been ploughed and rolled firm and flat. This is just about as good as it gets for us!

Walking across the field now, you feel like the ginger cat from next door on the seed tray in your greenhouse!

So from early in the year the field is growing until harvest time and this, depending on the crop, can be from late July (starting with the rape) through to September (with maize). This will also depend on the weather. Farmers hate to harvest wet crops as they have to spend good money drying them off. I organised a rally in 2008 and that year there was so much rain the crops were about four to six weeks late. I was lucky there was a dry spell the week before the rally, and most of the land was cropped and available on the day; but it was a close run thing!

EARPHONES KEEP OUT OTHER NOISES

However, both the farmer, and therefore us, are dependent on the weather; him for his living and us for our hobby. Sometimes a bit of rain will help us, as damp soil gives us a better signal response than dry conditions.

On some farms winter wheat (barley), is sown in late August or September to give it a head start before the winter arrives. This crop will then just stop growing and start again as soon as the weather improves in the spring. This winter crop gives the farmer a head start and should give a crop three to four weeks earlier than normal and it allows the farmer to spreads things out at his busiest time of the year. Of course, this means that throughout the winter these fields are out of bounds to you, but it's harvested earlier in the year so that's a bonus.

As soon as the crop is harvested, it's time to get out there as Mr. Farmer doesn't hang about. Some crops can now be drilled straight into the ground, with a minimum of preparation or, if you are luckier, it could be left until later.

Every farm is different and every farm can change its cycle from year to year. Years ago, land used to be left fallow (just not used) and this allowed animals to graze to improve the soil; but now we have fertilisers, man-made and natural, to do this job, so allowing all the land to be used every year.

There are certain crops that are grown just to improve the soil.

A rough, half ploughed field.

These are grown quickly and then ploughed in and, as they break down, they release nitrogen back into the soil and so improve the growing quality. This might give you another small window of opportunity. Added to this, farms generally change the crop cycle to stop bugs and disease taking hold, so after this year's maize the farmer might put in potatoes or wheat next year, and this will change your detecting cycle again. So basically knowing what is going on in the farm can help you plan your year, and how to make the best of every opportunity that might arise.

Weed control and fertilising can happen at any time, on any of the crops. So, if you see a tractor driving across a field of crops spraying liquid or solid pellets, don't assume you can detect - he has to be there, you don't.

All of these times are a guide, as climate change over the last 10 years or so has meant work on the farm has started earlier and earlier each year. This, combined with modern technology and more sophisticated and resistant crops, has led to a marked increase in the length of time land is unavailable to detectorists.

So with all the land types you might encounter, I am just going to list the fields in my preferred order. This might not be everybody's cup of tea, but these are what I prefer. With a good mix of types you should be able to detect right through the year!

- Ploughed disked, seeded and rolled field
- Maize seedlings growing
- Last year's barley/wheat stubble
- Freshly ploughed and rolled earth
- A harvested potato field
- A field ploughed and disked
- Maize stubble from last year

- Maize stubble new
- Freshly ploughed land
- Rape stubble (good for nothing)

There are of course other types of detecting fields in different parts of the country.

Rape stubble seems to be God's idea of a joke on us detectorists; not much is grown by my farmers, but when it is I just stay away as it's resilient to everything except the plough. Just walking through it can be a hard work!

Non-Arable Land

With non-arable land (that's grass to you and me) you don't get so many different conditions - but you do get different types, and length of grass from sheep lawns to thick well growing tussocks which are just not worth trying. In winter most grass stops growing, so it tends to be shorter, and you have a good few months to detect. Also at this time of the year, you don't get cattle out as they are normally in the sheds.

Most of the time, early in the growing season, grass will be allowed to grow with no animals on it; this is grown long for silage. When it's a good length Mr. Farmer will mow it and then allow it to dry in the field for a while then bag it into the large round black bales that you see in the fields. This will then be fed to cows later in the year. While it is laying drying on the ground in long rows it's a good opportunity to get out as he will always cut it as short as possible. This will give you long wide stretches to walk down; just perfect on a nice spring day!

A grass field that recently produced a hammered silver groat.

In the spring and summer grass that has had cattle on is fine to detect on most of the time, but you do have to watch where you put your feet! Fields

ALWAYS ONE EYE ON THE CATTLE

with sheep are really excellent; in fact they are as good as a fleet of lawnmowers and have more benign toilet habits! Also sheep have a tendency to move away from you, where cattle are much more inquisitive, and can be a nuisance, to say the least.

Always check with the farmer before you think about detecting in a field of cattle as they can be very unpredictable.

In a cattle field, one eye should be on the ground, and the other one on the cows. If you have a third eye that would be useful, as it could watch your back.

As with all animals you can become complacent very easily; there are many stories where even farmers have been maimed or killed because they thought they knew their animals, and took them for granted. With cows on the farm you can get bulls as well. Some farms raise them from calves to sell on. Think is it worth going in that particular field?

Let's talk bull - no, not this writing, but the big thing with horns on! I bet he can run faster than you and, as it's his home turf, I personally think he has an edge. I plan never to challenge him to a race! Remember he can be very dangerous.

You might also encounter horses, pigs, llamas, goats, alpacas, even bison; you never know what is going to be breathing down your neck! I have never tried detecting in a pig field (with or without them in residence) and I cannot imagine what it would be like. I was invited once, but I declined so if you ever go, please let me know what it was like - that is when you have had a wash or two.

Grass tends to stay in for about five or six years, then it will be ploughed in and then reseeded, or a completely different crop will be planted.

Footpaths

Footpaths are an integral part of the British countryside: they go together like fish and chips, like Yorkshires with roast beef. They cross the fields of Britain like a lace pattern. They have been essential for getting around our countryside for hundreds; maybe thousands of years and in this time people have dropped a multitude of items crossing from one field to the next. If you have one on your farm work it well, not just in a straight line; include both sides as they have moved over the years for all sorts of reasons, and the plough has moved more soil and finds than you can imagine.

But always remember: if you don't have permission to detect on that field you have no right to detect on that public footpath. You only have the right to cross the field, nothing else.

Quick Breakdown

So from early in the year you will have last year's stubble; then ploughed and rolled land, ready for seeding; then land being got ready for potatoes and maize. By this time the winter wheat is growing well, and the spring cereals are starting to sprout and the maize is going in earlier ever year. By July some rape crops are ripening well, and are soon out, with that year's crop following on. By August/September it's all hands to the pumps, and stubble is appearing everywhere, with maize coming along last. A quick plough and some fields are soon seeded. Grass can be available all year, but can sometimes be too long for detecting.

How To Detect

So you have your detector, digger, and sandwiches. You have permission from the farmer to be where you are; which is just inside the first field of your first farm. Now what? Well, it's time to find out if our great hobby is for you and to do that you need a few hints before you set off. The one thing you will need is a basic understanding of how to detect!

All anybody needs is a bit of common sense. Beginners might think that every long time detectorist they talk to is an expert - and might claim to be so. But that is not true in my case. After all my time in the hobby I have to admit that I am still learning!

Sometimes I am amazed at what I see detectorists doing in the name of metal detecting. This is always more obvious when you go to rallies and see people swinging their detectors all over the place, digging massive holes, and then not filling them properly. What is also appalling is the amount of rubbish that is dug up and then left on top of the ground. I once saw somebody leave 3 feet of rusty chain on the grass; can you imagine what that would have done to

WATCH YOUR SWING

the farmer's equipment as he cut and bailed the grass? People also carry spades big enough for a navvy - it does make you wonder!

It is also important that if you are detecting with others, give yourself a bit of space. Machines will interfere with each other and you really don't want to go crashing into other detectorists!

What we are trying to do here, is to help you get some of the knowledge that you will need to enjoy our hobby. So how do you start? The one thing you have to realise is there will always be targets out of range of whatever detector you have....it's a fact of life. This means you have to concentrate on the ones that *are* in the range of your detector.

To do this you have to detect in the right way and at the right speed, teach yourself to listen and identify the sounds in your headphones, and learn what your display (if you have one) is telling you.

Each make of detector reacts and sounds slightly different from another, and if you change your detector or your headphones, expect this.

Testing Your New Detector At Home

The parcel has at last arrived, and that first sight of your new detector lying in the box is very exciting. This is what you have been waiting for!

So let's do things right - first read the instructions on how to fit it together!

I say this as somebody who never reads instructions for anything. That normally means that I have to start again as things always seem to have a piece missing, they are of the wrong shape, or there are a lot of screws left over.

I tell the wife, "It's a manufacturing fault."

"It's funny you always seem to get the bad one," she says!

If you do run into problems, your supplier is only a phone call away, and they can talk you through it.

Hint: when fixing on the coil and its lead, don't wrap the lead too tightly around the stem, as you don't want it pulling on the connections; and try not to over-tighten the screw or thumb nuts!

By now you are okay with the instructions. You put a set of batteries in and switch it on. Doesn't it make a nice sound? If you have no sound at all, check the batteries are in the correct way!

A good pair of headphones are worth their weight in Iron Age gold staters. I believe you should always wear headphones as they will give you a better and clearer signal than the detector's in-built speaker. They cut down on background noise, and some specialist-designed detector headphones even amplify and boost the target signal.

Do you have long arms? If so, for a comfortable swing you are going to need the stem shorter than somebody with short arms. Your arm should be at an angle that doesn't pull on your shoulder, but you should still be able to rest the search head nearly on the ground. It might take a bit of getting used to, and a few weary arms, before you get it right.

Ground Balance

Some types of soil will give you false signals as a result of mineralisation. Machines can often counter this, and the "switch and go" machines will do this very easily indeed. They can then ignore any mineralisation in the soil and concentrate on the finding coins and artefacts. The manual for your machine will help you with this (so read it!), but if you intend to buy the detector from a shop then make sure you get a short lesson before you leave!

Discrimination

By far the most common metal object in the soil is an iron nail. Most detectors have an "all metal" setting and if you use this on your field, then you will dig up lots and lots of iron. This is fun for a bit but after a while you might like to introduce some discrimination. As each type of metal gives a different response, the machine will be able to ignore iron if you tell it to and most detectorists will do this. Different machines have different modes of discrimination, but the golden rule is to use as little as you can get away with. To be sure you might still dig up some iron but you will miss fewer non-ferrous items and, as a bonus, you get a little more depth from your machine. You will find that ringed iron objects, or those with a large hole in, tend to trick the discrimination and you will dig them anyway. So start low on 2-3; if you are digging unwanted small iron turn it up a little more until a signal from a large rusty nail starts to break up.

Threshold Sound

This is the small hum that you can hear in the background. This, if you have the facility on your detector, should be set so you can only just hear it as a target signal will sound over it. Some detectors go silent briefly as you pass over an iron target (like a small nail). This is normal and is called blanking out.

Swing

This is the easiest bit and the hardest to do correctly. The first rule is to keep the detecting head flat to the ground. The worst mistake people make is lifting the head at the end of the swing - so remember this isn't golf! You don't want to be hitting the ground hard, but the odd scuff is far better than missing the soil by several inches. The head is protected by a cover, that's what it's there for! The head should travel in a slight curve round to the right and left, and this can help to stop the head lifting at the each end of the swing.

A good steady swing, keeping the search head flat.

As I am right handed, my swing starts on the left side of the clock about "10 minutes to", and ends on my right about quarter past. Then, as I take a step forward, the head swings back. If you raise the head at the end of each swing you will not be getting the same depth as in the middle. So, for example, if your detector detects 4 inches down, as you raise your detector head, this will fall to perhaps 2 inches; so for a 3 feet swing the middle gets maximum depth and, at the end, a lot less.

This might equate to a loss of a quarter of the ground depth you should be covering with every swing that you make! The plus side of this is if there is an artefact hovering one inch above the ground you will find it, but it's a pity about the gold stater in the ground a little further down!

Your detector head should be kept moving. It's better to be slightly slow than fast on the swing, as this gives the machine time to react to a find and tell you, by sound and a visual display, what it is. The swing of your arm should be in time with the opposite leg, so your walking pace also, to a certain extent, determines your swing. Walk slowly, swing with each pace steadily, and keep the sweep speed constant.

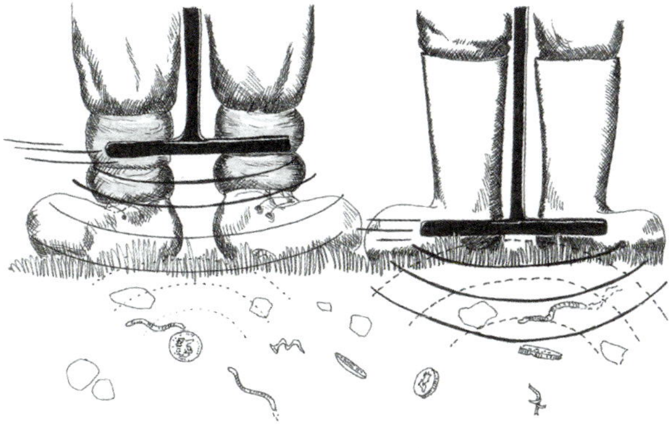

SEARCH HEAD SHOULD JUST MISS THE GROUND AT ALL TIMES

How To Detect

Sounds

Each and every detector will make different sounds for different objects. Sounds will alter for different types of metal, different depths, and even different sized objects. This is one of the things that you must get used to and the best way to start is to lay out different items on your lawn, and pass the head over each one in turn to listen to the sounds they produce.

"To Dig Or Not To Dig?"

If you dig every squeak or half-hearted beep from your machine, you will need a handcart to take your rubbish home, but if you only dig the really strong signals you might miss many good finds. A nice hammered coin just under the head will give you a different sound to the same one buried, at a slant, 4 inches down.

Only time spent with your detector, and learning the different types of signal it produces will give you the knowledge and experience to second guess the 'iffy' signals. So when you start, "if in doubt, dig it" and learn what different things sound like; and, if it's rubbish, take it home. At least then you are not missing anything and you're learning about your machine! As you get more experienced you will get less junk and what you do dig will be a better class of rubbish!

Pinpointing & Digging

You have a positive signal, but what do you do next? Do you get out the pick and shovel? No. First, check the signal by moving slightly around it and, if it doesn't disappear, switch to pinpoint mode (all metal). Now, as all detectors are slightly different, you might have to push a button, flick a switch up or down, or pull a switch towards you. (Chapter 3 will give you an insight into a few machines.) The pinpoint mode will help you determine precisely where your find is; normally the pitch will rise as the item gets to the centre of the search head. This will give you a straight line on the ground, about 6-8 inches long. Now move round at right angles to this and sweep again; the target is to be found where these two lines cross.

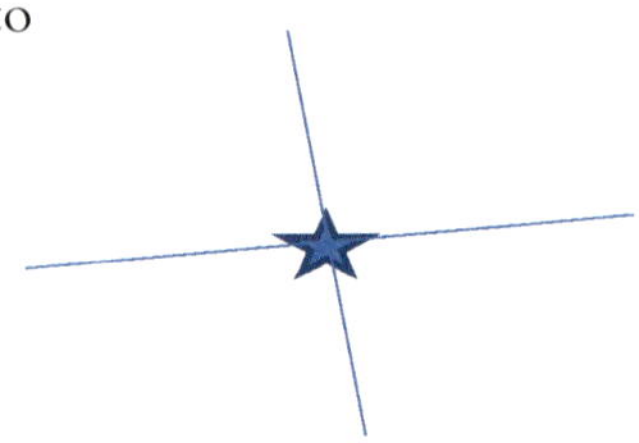

So after pinpointing the target, and you are sure you know where it is, all you have to do is dig it up! This sounds simple, but you have to do this correctly as you want to be able to dig the hole, take out the object, refill the hole, and not leave a mess.

The target should be right in the middle of that imaginary

cross. Start at least 4 inches away and slightly behind it, sliding your spade in straight down at least 4 inches to cut through the grass and the roots. Then pull back on the handle slightly (this will release the grass on that side). Now, depending on the size of your digger, cut again at a slight angle. Turn slightly and then do the same again, and then one parallel to your first cut; each time levering it slightly. So you now have four or five cuts, with one end still intact. This uncut end will act as a hinge on the grass, and is important as it will allow the grass to carry on growing afterwards without any damage.

The red star marks the target. Always dig at least 4 inches away.

With my small lady's spade I can make a cut like this and, with my fourth cut, I can lever back the grass flap. If you want a slightly bigger hole, use five cuts, but still leave the end intact. Then, by gently levering up this side, the whole piece will flap back, leaving the hole open with the 4 inch thick turf square on its back.

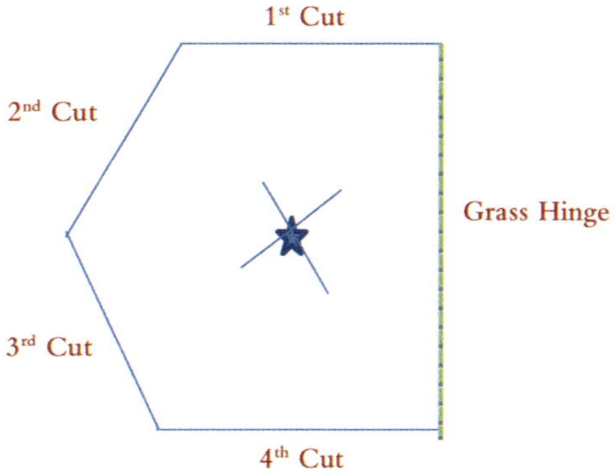

What you have now is a nearly square hole approximately 4 inches deep, and a piece of turf grass side down. The first thing to do is run your detector over the flap of grass to check if the target is in there; if it's not then check the open hole. Quite often it is lying just there, but sometimes you are going to have to dig a little more.

If the object was in the grass flap then this is where a probe comes in handy, as you can pinpoint it and carefully work out its location without damaging the turf square. The less harm you do to this square of grass, the less damage you are going to leave showing and the happier the landowner will be.

If your target is not in the grass flap it will be in the hole! First, check with your probe to see if your find is close to one of the edges. If it is, then you can carefully work it out with the tip of your knife. If it's deeper, then it is time to be really careful! Dig straight down again with the back of the spade against one side and carefully lever out the soil. If it's really hard compacted soil, it would be better if you release each side again before levering it out. Place this spadeful carefully in a pile next to the hole, checking each time for the find.

Some detectorists carry a square of plastic to put the dirt on; I always use this method on other people's lawns.

A nicely cut hole that will leave no mess.

So now you've found it! Perhaps it is an old coin, button, brooch, buckle, ring pull, or even a gold coin! A nice coin or artefact goes into your finds bag, either in its own plastic bag or a box. All the normal common, but interesting, bits that are not rubbish go into a safe bag or compartment. Rubbish (if you're sure it is) goes into your separate pouch or bag to be disposed of later (after a final check!). Before filling in the hole, check that there is not a second signal there. If it's a piece of trash take it home to dispose of it. There is no point in leaving it in the hole; you are only going to find it next year.

Some items of rubbish can be recycled, so do your bit for the environment!

Now carefully put all the loose dirt and stones back into the hole, and flap back the turf. Then gently firm it down with your foot, until it's the same as the grass around it. Finally, with your gloved hand, sweep away any loose dirt. Your hole should then be practically invisible, and the grass will quickly recover and continue growing.

The hole filled in and with no mess left on top.

If you are detecting on a stubble field it's not so important how tidy you are at filling your hole in, but the same care should always be used to dig the hole.

Always refill it! Never leave a hole open, as it could be a danger to animals or people walking or riding across the land. And always remove any rubbish you dig!

Large and heavy chunks of iron etc. should be disposed of safely by taking them home.

Recording Finds

We will mention more about recording finds later, and the reasons why we need to do so. Always make a note of where you found a particular item. Once at home, as you empty your rubbish bag, double check. If necessary, wash an item to ensure it is rubbish before you dispose of it. Anything you are not sure of, save and ask for help with identification at your club meeting - if you belong to one - or the help of more experienced detectorists. A lot of the bits of metal can be recycled (why put it in landfill?). In the Trowbridge Club we collect all the lead, sell it, and give the money to a charity.

Farm Watch

Farm Watch (similar to Neighbourhood Watch) is an organisation that helps to stop crime in the countryside. You can also help by having the number of your farmer and the Farm Watch scheme on your mobile. Then, if you see anything suspicious, or out of the ordinary, you can give your farmer a ring. It could be your car next time. One of our members had a bag stolen from the hedgerow where he had hid it. He found it later burnt to a crisp, with his spare detector head still in it. Another member used his phone when he found a herd of cows had got into the maize field; one of our farmers really appreciated that call!

Gold Aureus

One of the best stories I have ever heard was where one detectorist had been going back occasionally to the same, well-worked site for over 30 years, convinced that there were more Roman bits to be found. Then, one day, he found a magnificent gold coin. For me this is as good as it gets, and it is a Roman *aureus* of Domitian, who was murdered in AD 96.

This just proves what we always say: there is no such thing as a worked out site, just well worked, which is quite different! Every year, when the top soil is turned by the plough, the earth moves left, right or forward. Objects are never in the same position twice. Thirty years is a long time for a hobby, but not for one as interesting as this. You just never know what you are going to find.

A Final Thought

Should you go slowly and overlap each swing to ensure you miss nothing? Or should you walk at a reasonable pace, and not cover every inch of ground?

By overlapping you might find everything that is in front of you, but it's going to take you longer than your mate to cover the same amount of ground as him.

Two detectorists, Fred and George, using the same size search head at the same speed of swing will cover different amounts of ground. Fred might only cover half the distance of George but he will get maximum depth over a smaller piece of land; whereas George will certainly cover a greater distance but at slightly less depth, and not as thoroughly.

They are both wrong, and both right for different reasons.

There used to be a saying "a miss is as good as a mile". The reality is, if you are an inch out, then you could miss a target. To get that maximum depth you are going to have to overlap each of your swings, which means it's going to take you twice as long to cover the same amount of ground!

If you are going to do this methodically you should be detecting between two rows of string so you don't miss anything. By stringing a section a 3 feet wide, and overlapping you will know that you have done that piece of ground thoroughly, and you have not missed a thing within range of your detector. So if George misses a target, he will not know that he has missed it, and Fred will never know what he might have got as he will never reach the other side of the field! It's entirely up to you!

New For Old

When I was a boy a tanner was sixpence; a bob was a shilling; and half a crown was two bob and a tanner. So now 3 feet is about 1 metre, and 4 inches is about 10 centimetres.

What You Can Find - Coins

We are now going to look at the items that are possible to find when you go out detecting. These are going to range from coins to buttons; buckles to badges; rings to rubbish: good, bad and indifferent. It's all out there for you to find, all it takes is a willingness to put in the time, and to learn as you go along. Man's imagination to use the technology available to him, and to turn out objects that he needed and then lost, means that we can now find these items from all those years ago.

The use of modern technology and modern farming methods, such as chemicals and fertilisers on the fields, are making some of these items corrode away at a much faster rate than ever before. This means that it is very important for us to find and record items before they disintegrate in the soil; we really are saving our nation's heritage.

6,000 Years Of Finds

This is what it is all about. This is our hobby, and these finds will make you ecstatic, bored, mad, crazy, or pleased - probably all in the same day. In this chapter I am going to show some of the different metal items that it is possible to find.

People living in this country have been losing their metal objects for over 4,000 years. It starts with Bronze Age axe heads, the Celts and their staters, and then 400 years of the Roman occupation. We then saw the Saxon raiders come and settle and Scandinavian Vikings, in the North, also left their goods buried for us to find. The medieval period, right across the country, saw vast changes in what people owned and subsequently lost. The Tudors followed, and Elizabeth I seemed to produce the most silver coins to be found of any monarch; they are found in their thousands each and every year. The Civil War, between the Cavaliers and Roundheads, saw some fantastic coins of all shapes going into the fields. Throughout the 17th, 18th, and 19th centuries, machine-made coinage and artefacts were scattered about in ever increasing numbers. Each generation of our ancestors has produced a different variety of items for us to find, and we can uncover a small part of their lives when we dig these objects.

Assorted low value coins.

Coins

Before mentioning anything, let me say that you should as a priority get yourself a copy of a good coin catalogue, such as Spink's *Coins of England and the UK* or, if you live north of the border, the Scottish equivalent. The values they give for coins may, or may not, be of interest to you (remember that FLOs are not allowed to give valuations) but as a means to identifying any coins you find they are essential and worth every penny. Even a book such as Spink's catalogue is merely a general introduction, and if you get particularly involved in coins you will need to buy some more specialist volumes, particularly for Roman and Celtic coins.

So we first come to the thorny question of what exactly was a coin for? Can we assume that a silver coin in the 18th century had a similar function as one produced in the early 1st century? Well, it is not for the likes of us to answer that one but it is an interesting thought, and we should not make simple assumptions about the world 2,000 years ago! One point that we can safely make is that, until the 20th century, the value of a coin was based on the value of the metal from which it was made; however, that is just not true anymore. A £1 coin is only "worth" that because I trust that I can use it to get £1's worth of stuff at a shop; but the metal itself as scrap might only be worth a few pence. That was emphatically not the case in the past, and it is a line of investigation that I will come back to later on.

Jettons, tokens and coin weights are not coins, and should always be considered artefacts. So what I intend to do here is merely guide you through some examples of the sort of genuine coins you might just find - the most general of general introductions! All the coins shown have been found by members of our club and are reproduced with permission.

Late Iron Age

If you are talking history, the term "Celtic" is unhelpful and

increasingly controversial; it is much better to talk of the "late Iron Age". But with coins you just can't escape the word and so, reluctantly, I will refer to Celtic coins and hope I don't get told off by any passing historian. Now I'd better own up as I've never even found a Celtic coin, although one is high on my wish list; but they do turn up and you may well be luckier than me. Only, that is, if you happen to live in the parts of Britain dotted in the sketch map. It shows a distribution of all Iron Age objects recorded with the PAS and the bias is clear. So if Devonshire or Cornwall is your patch - or Wales, the North West or anywhere in Scotland - then I fear it is just not going to happen without some long distance travelling to potential sites being involved.

They are coins like no other, are usually made of silver or gold, and have the most beautiful abstract designs, often involving horses. Even the names are strange: "staters", "quarter staters", and silver or bronze "units". The world of Celtic coinage is technical and complex, and much about them is still not understood.

The first coins made in Britain come from about 100 BC, although it seems that imports from Gaul (France) existed before that time. Regional tribes each had their own coinage and, in a time with no written records, the type and distribution of these coins can tell us much about political boundaries and trade about which we would otherwise be ignorant. Indeed, such tribal identity may even stretch across the Channel with identical coin types often found in, what is now modern Belgium or Northern France. With the Roman Conquest of Britain in AD 43, the brief flourishing of Celtic currency came to a sudden end.

Silver stater.

The right hand example has a stylised horse, facing right, over a chariot wheel on the bottom, which is a quite common motif. In the top right hand quarter is a design that looks, to me at least, a bit like a torc (such as those found in the famous Snettisham Hoard). The reverse on some Celtic coins is simply blank!

Different sides of two staters.

What You Can Find - Coins

Celtic stater.

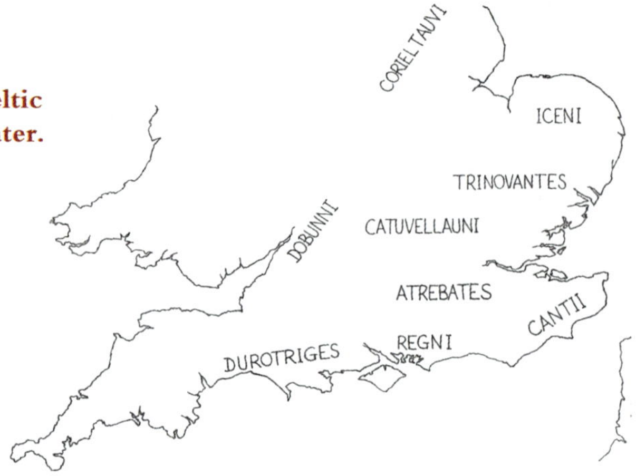

In the second example, above, which has a diameter of 10mm, the horse is facing left but still straddles the wheel, and has a stylised head of Apollo on the other side.

Another iconic image to appear on these coins is a sheaf of wheat. It seems probable that horses, chariots and agricultural production were the symbols and reality of power for these pre-Roman societies. Of course, the examples shown look totally different from modern coins because they lack any writing or a representation of an individual ruler.

In the years before the Roman invasion proper, and as Roman influence inevitably grew, this began to slowly change. For the first time in British history we have the names of people appearing on some coins, which began to evolve a more Romanised feel to them.

What were the territories of these Celtic tribes? The sketch gives a rough idea and by recording any coins you find you will help the academics get a better sense of what was going on in this mysterious period.

Roman Coins (AD 43-c.350)

For this period, of about 300 years or so, coins are found in huge numbers and just about everywhere (in stark contrast to what followed in the 5th and 6th centuries). The nature of trade and the construction of roads for the movement of goods, all meant that a coin-based economy developed. The coins themselves set the standard for all those that followed, and look much more like modern coinage than the Iron Age examples above ("Britannia", still found on the older 50p piece, first appeared on Roman coins). The emperor, or occasionally his wife, appears on the obverse, which gives the coin authority and also serves as a political statement for the ruler himself; a reminder that any wealth you might possess was dependent on the goodwill of the guy whose face was on your coins!

Roman serrated *denarius.*

Roman coinage is a massive and rather daunting subject, and there are hundreds and hundreds of different coin variants and many different denominations that themselves varied over the centuries. Specialist coin books are listed at the back of this book; but don't go rushing into the bookshop until you've established, at least the beginnings of, a collection. You might just come across a coin that predates the invasion which, we can speculate, came across to these islands because of trade. These belong to the "Republican" period of Roman history (up to 27 BC), and look quite a bit different from those that followed. This silver Republican *denarius* has a serrated edge (a *serratus*) the purpose of which is, as I understand it, still unknown.

Two silver Roman *denarii.*

After the Roman invasion coins were imported into Britain from mints all over the Empire and it can be fascinating to find out where some of the coins you find were actually made. Some were officially minted here, usually in London, but later on unofficial coins appeared in large quantities. Between the invasion and about AD 250 there were five types of coin as listed below.

- The *aureus* (literally means gold). If you are lucky enough to find one of these coins, you have my permission to go dancing down the street! They are very rare indeed.
- The *denarius* (penny, plural *denarii*), was originally solid silver but like those below later ones can be merely silver "washed" meaning that they are copper coins with a thin coating of silver on top. We still used the word for our pennies until decimalisation in 1971 (i.e.1d).
- The *siliqua* (plural *siliquae*) was solid silver. The mint marks are at the base of the reverse (e.g. Constantinople and Trier in these cases).
- The *sestertius* was a big, heavy copper-alloy coin. Some of these can be quite worn as they were in circulation for a long time.

Silver *siliquae.*

• The *dupondius* and the *as* (now don't laugh, this is a serious business) were smaller copper-alloy coins. I, for one, am not very good at telling them apart.

By the middle of the 3rd century, the coins above had pretty much disappeared and were replaced with coins that we call "radiates". The name comes from the spiky looking crown which actually represents the sun's rays. These coins are extremely common finds on the fields of England and cover a period of between c.AD 215 to the end of the 3rd century. (These were the coins that made up the Frome Hoard, with only five *denarii* in with them.) Early radiates had significant silver content, but with time (and possibly inflation?) they became smaller and increasingly coppery. Many home-made copies of radiates were produced, called "barbarous radiates", although it is not easy to know to what extent these were officially sanctioned or just blatant forgeries.

A debased Roman silver radiate.

The example on the right is a "silver washed" radiate, and you can see how the thin layer has worn away showing the copper alloy beneath.

In the 4th century the coinage changed again and a range of new copper-alloy coins appeared, collectively termed *nummi* (singular *nummus*).

Bronze Roman *nummus*.

The *nummus* on the right is of Constantius II and dates to AD 348-350. The reverse is quite dramatic (to me at least) as it seems to show a soldier leading a child to safety and away from a building on fire! I think that the reverse images on some Roman coins can be much more fascinating than the bust of the emperor on the obverse.

Before we leave Roman Britain, please don't be fooled by the photographs above. Although it is possible to find coins in excellent condition, most coins will be small and grotty; indeed we call them exactly that - "grots". The coin below right is typical of those I find, and is by far not the worst! Some will be barely recognisable as coins and you may not even be able to make out the bust, let alone any writing. However, these too, should be recorded with the PAS, as they also have their story to tell.

Roman coin in poor condition.

"Roman coins make up the vast majority (64%) of coins recorded (and this total excludes coins found in hoards, such as the Frome hoard of 52,503 coins) - it is the largest open-access database of Roman coins in the world. Because so many Roman coins have been found it is not surprising that a significant number of unrecorded types and new varieties have come to light. In this way, detector finds are adding significantly to our knowledge of Roman coinage in general. This is especially the case with coins struck in Britain by the usurpers Carausius and Allectus (AD 286-96) and for coins struck at London which was a mint from 286 to 325.

"The new edition of the *Roman Imperial Coinage* for Carausius and Allectus will contain a large number of previously unknown coins recorded with the PAS. Furthermore, future volumes of RIC covering the Tetrarchy and House of Constantine (AD 296-325) will contain a number of new London mint coins. However, the PAS probably provides the largest corpus of new material for contemporary copies of Roman coins, mostly made in Britain. We have added about 600 Claudian period copies, over 1,000 Severan period copies of *denarii*, and many thousands of radiate and *nummus* copies of the late 3rd and 4th centuries. This enormous dataset of "irregular" coins will provide future researchers with the largest known corpus of contemporary copies from Britain.

In addition, the PAS has recorded a significant number of Roman gold coins which are included in a recent book. The data is also changing our understanding of late Roman silver coinage in Britain. Finally, almost 100 Byzantine coins have been recorded, overturning the view that Byzantine coins were all lost in the modern period.

"In addition to new numismatic data, the recording of Roman coins is leading to a national picture of Roman activity. Because so many detectorists have been showing us their "grots", there are over 900 parishes from which more than 20 Roman coins have been recorded; a few have over a thousand! In many cases these assemblages represent new Roman sites and in some counties our knowledge of Roman settlement has been changed greatly - for example on the Isle of Wight and in Devon.

"Furthermore, by analysing the chronological spread and density of the coins we are able to make preliminary assessments about the date range of occupation at particular sites. Such studies can be expanded to show regional patterns - for example, Philippa Walton has shown that in the southern and eastern parts of Britain, 3rd and

4th century coins are most common; in the Northern and western parts of the country, there is a relatively higher proportion of 1st and 2nd century coins."
(Sam Moorhead, National Finds Advisor for Roman & Iron Age Coins, Department of Portable Antiquities and Treasure in the British Museum.)

Saxon & Viking Coinage

You were probably taught at school that the Romans left Britain in the mid-4th century and the Angles, Saxons and Jutes (in Kent) took over. But only when you have detected for a few years does it hit home what a cataclysmic change this represented. Early Saxon coins are as rare as hen's teeth, and although coinage makes a recovery in the late 13th century, and again in the time of Elizabeth, it is only in the 18th century, and the dawn of the Industrial Revolution, that I would say that coins finds are as common as those from the Roman period. That is quite a thought!

No coins at all reappear in England until the middle of the 7th century. I say "England", but the reality of that word was still a couple of hundred years away and instead we had a series of separate petty kingdoms which spent most of the time fighting one another. From the cauldron of those related power centres such as East Anglia, Northumbria, Kent, Mercia and Wessex and, most importantly perhaps, the external Viking threat, would grow a nation; but let's not get ahead of ourselves.

Early Saxon coins, called sceattas and pronounced "skeets", were small (less than 1cm in diameter), and tried to imitate Roman currency. The designs were copies of copies of Roman coins and became quite abstract and unrecognisable. By the late 8th and early 9th centuries, silver coins were being minted which were larger, of better quality, and clearly the forebears of the later medieval coinage. Names of rulers were clearly shown on coins. Any Saxon coin is a wonderful and valuable find (I've never found one) and I personally think the later ones are quite beautiful.

This is a silver penny of Aethelstan, King of Wessex between AD 924 and 939. He was the grandson of Alfred the Great and managed to unite all of England and much of Scotland under his rule. This coin is in absolutely wonderful condition and (don't tell you know who) I would rather find this single object than a Roman hoard!

Saxon silver penny of Aethelstan.

On the right is a rare "cut half" of Eadmund, Aethelstan's younger brother, and King of Wessex between AD 939 and 946; a lovely find, but still a shame that it wasn't complete.

Saxon cut penny of Eadmund.

Of course, all coins from the Iron Age to Charles II were made by hand (okay, not quite true, but almost) and are called "hammered" coins. These were made by inserting a blank silver disc between two, much harder, steel dies for the obverse and reverse images, and whacking it with a great big hammer to make the impressions. Lots of things could go wrong with this; for example, the silver disc might not be central to the die and the image would not be in the middle of the coin. Or, perhaps after a heavy night out, the guy with the hammer might use too little force and the image appears weak. You even see coins with a double image, where there had been two attempts at getting it right! These will always detract from the appeal of the coin to a modern collector and, hence, its value, but not to the interest from the detectorist.

Until the time of the recoinage of Edward I, in 1279, it was usual for the name of the moneyer to appear on the coin. This was the person who, while not actually wielding the hammer, was responsible to the king for the quality of coinage coming from the mint. By putting your name on the coin you could hardly hide any deficiencies! Of course, in a pre-industrial age there was a limit to how many coins any one mint could produce and so they opened up (and often closed down) in major towns across the country throughout the medieval period; and it usually possible to identify where your coin was made.

Medieval Period

The medieval period I will take, for the purposes of this chapter, to be 1066 to the demise of Richard III in 1485.

Early medieval silver penny.

Coins of the first Norman kings are very rare and you might detect for 25 years and never find one. The only coin in existence was the silver penny and this, and the political instability in the country, presumably did not encourage trade based on coinage. By the time of Henry II (1154-1189) things had eased a little and larger numbers of very poorly made silver pennies appear. They are called "Tealby" pennies after a hoard of 5,000 found in Lincolnshire in 1807. Why they are of such bad quality I have no idea, but there it is.

What You Can Find - Coins

Clipped part of a James I half groat.

One reason that hammered coins (usually!) had to be well made was to avoid clipping. Remember that the coin's value was based on the metal from which it was made. So, unscrupulous traders would take small shavings, or clippings, off the coins that passed through their hands, hoping that the customer would be too busy to notice. This would provide a handy little side line and illicit profit! Of course this was strictly illegal and the penalties could be severe. However, detectorists regularly find clipped hammered coins, so it obviously went on as can be seen on this half groat (2d) of James I. If a coin is usually a perfect circle it is easier to notice where a little has been removed and you can simply refuse to accept it. If good and bad coins come your way, then you are more likely to spend the clipped ones (if you can get away with it), and keep the perfect ones. If everyone does that, then the coins in actual circulation get rapidly worse in quality, and confidence is lost in their value. Numismatists call this Gresham's Law (i.e. that bad coinage drives out good). Eventually this could have had an adverse effect on medieval economic growth and for the state became a serious issue. So every now and then there would be a recoinage, with bright new shiny coins replacing the old corrupted ones, assuming the new silver was available. At the same time, the design of the coins would be improved to try and make clipping more obvious.

On the right is the short cross penny, brought in by Henry II in 1180 to replace the Tealby penny. Its innovation was to encourage use of coin by allowing "small change" to be created. The double-lined cross meant that when it was cut into halves or quarters; one line of the cross visibly showed it had been done fairly (see right, although this is a slightly later coin) or even quarters. So literally "half-pennies" or "fourth-things" (later called farthings) could be made for use in the local market. It might not be that clear from the image, but the obverse starts by spelling HENRICVS, which is fair enough you might think. Alas the coins hardly changed for the next three kings, so HENRICVS it stubbornly remains for Richard I, John and Henry III! If you want to identify these then record them and get the museum to do it for you!

Short cross penny.

It was Henry III who, in 1247, introduced the long cross penny where, on the reverse, the cross was extended to the edge of the coin. This was to try and

Long cross, with arms of cross going right to the edge.

reduce clipping and improve the quality of money in circulation. In 1279, in a major recoinage, Edward I took it a stage further and had the long cross splayed at the end (so it was clear where the coin edge should be). The difference between the short and long cross is obvious from these two coins. The lower coin is a penny of Edward II, and was minted in Durham, land of the Prince Bishops, as can be seen by the top part of the cross which is actually a bishop's mitre!

A later long cross, ends of cross splayed.

The country was becoming richer and the number of coins that detectorists find rapidly increases with Edward I and his immediate successors. It is far from easy to tell which Edward you have on your coin as the rather two dimensional portraits look quite similar and, unhelpfully, the coins just say "Edward". Worse still, we are still 200 years away from some bright spark having the idea of including dates. One useful guide is to look at the lettering and if you see a lower case "n", called Lombardic script, then it is probably Edward II (1307-1327). An upper case "N" could mean Edward I, as could "EDWR" at the start, whereas "EDWA" would be Edward II or III. Another good tip is to look at the crown, which consists of a central part and two side pieces. Ignore the centre and just look at the side; if it is in three small divisions, trifoliate, then it suggests Edward I, whereas a bifoliate division is likely to be Edward II.

As for Edward III (1327-1377), look for the "pop star" hair, like this one on the right. It's much bushier than for Edwards I or II. The reverse inscription reads CIVI TAS LON DON, meaning that it was minted in the Tower of London. The obverse starts with a cross (at 12 o'clock) then EDWA [R AN] GLoDNSHyB which, roughly translated, means "Edward King of England and Lord of Ireland".

Silver Edward III penny.

A proper reference book will give you a full list of medieval mints and when they operated but, just to whet your appetite, here are a few of the more common:

York.................. CIVI TAS EBO RACI
Durham .... CIVI TAS DUN ELM
Canterbury......... CIVI TAS CAN TOR
Calais .... VILLA CALESIE

For the majority of the population there was a desperate need for smaller denominations. Cut halves and farthings were gradually replaced by properly minted smaller coins. At the same time, quite beautiful larger coins were made with the groat (4d) appearing along with the half groat (2d); the word meaning "great" coin. Having a wide range of denominations provided a stimulus to trade, and at the top end gold coins made a return to England, not that your average peasant would ever see one, and neither, unless you are very lucky, will you!

Silver groat from the Calais mint.

Tudor & Stuart Hammered Coins

The design of English coins remained largely unchanged for 200 years. It was not until Henry Tudor, a Welshman with a weak claim to the throne, emerged triumphant from the protracted War of the Roses, and became an unlikely Henry VII, did the style begin to change. With his son, the infamous Henry VIII, there was major reform (notice the profile bust of the Henry VIII groat on the right, and the new heraldic shield on the reverse). Most importantly, and controversially, was the devaluing of coinage. In an effort to pay for his foreign wars, and his extravagant lifestyle, Henry VIII did what all the medieval monarchs had resisted and reduced the silver content of the coins by alloying them with copper. Indeed he became known as "Old Coppernose" because it was said, that shortly after minting, the first hint of wear would rub the silver off his nose revealing the copper underneath. This debasement gave him a short term financial boost, (the modern equivalent is quantitative easing – nothing changes!) but it simply pushed up inflation making people poorer and was very unpopular.

Silver groat of Henry VIII.

His daughter, Elizabeth, when she came to the throne, tried to put things right and issued coinage with a higher purity of silver. Elizabethan hammered coins are, by some way, the most common to be found and she produced a bewildering variety of coin denominations. Perhaps due to the length of her reign, the coins are often pretty tatty when we recover them, but you might be lucky! On the right is a shilling found very recently and it is in stunning condition.

We now have dates, on most coins at least, and the Tudor Rose to the right of the bust on every other denomination - no doubt to help people more easily identify the coins. An odd feature of Elizabethan coins is that the queen's bust is commonly more worn than the reverse. I have heard it said that this is because rubbing the head with your thumb brought good luck! Did people really think that at the time? I have no idea, but it's a nice story!

Elizabeth I shilling.

On the left a genuine coin, on the right a poor forgery.

The two coins above illustrate an interesting point about currency of all periods. On the left is a genuine "Lizzie" sixpence of 1578, but that on the right, dated 1569, is a contemporary forgery. It is physically a bit smaller (24mm diameter not 26mm), the silver looks to be debased, and the quality of the die is much lower – look at the reverse shield on both and see the difference! If you find a coin, of any period, that "looks wrong" then there just might be a reason for it!

Moving to the 17th century, and the last few decades of the handmade hammered coin, the shilling (12d) of Charles I, right, looks very similar in design to the sixpence above. Annoyingly, we've lost the date, but gained the denomination in Roman numerals and this continues in the half groat (2d) of the Commonwealth, below right. This coin shows the emblems of England and Ireland, but any trace of a monarch (or Scotland for that matter) is missing. During the Civil War, very odd looking, and rare, "siege money" was issued from royalist towns such as Carlisle or Newark but, sadly, I think that's a little beyond the scope of this book!

Charles I shilling.

Commonwealth period half groat.

Milled Coins

With Charles II onwards, coins were machine made, "milled", and look much more familiar to us. The thicker edges to these machined coins gave Sir Isaac Newton, of all people, as Master of the Royal Mint the opportunity to introduce those little ridges, still with us today, that once and for all got rid of the medieval scourge of "clipping". The other great change was the mass introduction of copper alloyed coins, although this occurred in fits and starts right until the early 19th century. Inflation had increased the value of silver and the size of a silver penny, or still worse a halfpenny, was now just too small to be practical. The only sensible solution was to have copper coinage and, as the 18th century progressed, the Industrial Revolution and the increased population in the towns, who needed to be paid, made the problem far more immediate. The patchy response of the state to these demands led to several waves of unofficial copper coinage (see the bit about jettons and tokens below) but when proper coinage was minted it was done so in very large numbers, and these are some of the most common coins that you will find.

On the right is a halfpenny of George I, dated 1721. These coins, from William III through to George III, seem to be much more common than the larger penny and, judging from the often much worn condition of the coins that we find, were in circulation for many years. To the right are halfpennies from George II (1731) and George III (1773). You can see that the direction of the bust alternates with each monarch (it still does) and this can be helpful in identifying badly worn coins.

Halfpenny of George I.

Halfpennies of George II and George III.

A common, if slightly mysterious, find is an 18th century coin which has been deliberately bent into having an "S" profile. We often describe them as love tokens, but quite how they were used I really don't know. Perhaps they were buried by the loving couple; perhaps thrown away after a row! The one illustrated is a bent George III halfpenny, but they are often made out of worn silver coins.

George III halfpenny made into a love token.

Another deformed coin is this George II halfpenny which has had a crude rim added. I have seen several of these and can only assume it was to allow them to be rolled in some sort of game.

George III halfpenny with crude rim added.

Although pennies crop up less frequently in this period, an exception is the "cartwheel" penny of 1797. These were produced by George III to rid the country

George IV silver shilling.

George VI penny.

of unofficial tokens, but they were bulky, heavy and unpopular. A pocketful of these would have certainly weighed you down!

Throughout the 19th century, coins became perfectly manufactured and, in the 20th century, gradually less important as paper money took over. After the First World War, the silver content of "silver coins" became less and less until, today, it is zero. Indeed, the copper content in "coppers" went the same way until today they too are largely copper free. The value of the metal in modern coinage is only a small fraction of the face value and exchange is based on trust, although I am informed that perhaps 5% of pound coins in circulation are counterfeit – some things do not change!

Although coins from the last 200 years or so are unlikely to be rare or valuable, and your FLO will not be interested in them, they can still be good finds. The George IV shilling, from 1829, and even the George VI penny, from 1938 (above), are in such lovely condition that I still think of them as some of my best coins, and another seasoned member of our club once told me that his favourite coin of all was a Victorian sixpence!

But I cannot bring myself to finish our brief survey with a copper penny, however nice it may be. Maybe, just maybe, if you make a very powerful wish over your birthday candles, you may find a gold coin. I never have, but some do and, so you might recognise the colour, I present two coins found by friends of mine, both guineas - the first a guinea of James II dated 1688 (right), and the other a guinea of George III dated 1775 (below).

Gold guinea of James II.

Gold guinea of George III.

What You Can Find - Artefacts

What is an artefact? Basically anything that isn't a coin! The variety of objects that you find tells you everything about the wealth of the society that lost them. Throughout history, if you had money, then you spend it on "stuff" and it is no surprise that the greatest variety of metal objects we find date from the Roman period, and then from the Industrial Revolution onwards. Artefacts can be much more personal than coins and, as some detectorists argue, bring you closer to the people who owned them.

Brooches, Badges, Pendants & Mounts

This is a broad topic and many of the objects that I will look at do not sit that well in each other's company; but at least we can look at a wide range of objects in one section!

The heyday of brooches was in the very late Iron Age and early Roman period. The top example is from the late Iron Age and has a style described as Le Tène. Like some of the later Roman examples, to modern eyes this is a glorified safety pin, although I'm not sure that is a fair description of such a beautiful object! It has a lovely green patina and understated decoration. It is elegant in the extreme and would not look out of place in the 1920s. These seem to be Celtic interpretations of Roman brooches that were, presumably, appearing through trade.

The Roman example, lower right, is lovely in its own way but the decoration is a little less free

Celtic brooch.

Roman brooch with pin intact.

Roman brooch with fine inlaid enamel decoration.

flowing and more, well ... Roman. You can clearly see the catch plate for the pin.

Some fields will give large numbers of these bow brooches and, given that they broadly fell out of fashion by the end of the 2nd century; that might tell you something about the site. These two examples also show the difference between a hinged pin (bottom) and a sprung pin (top). Nine times out of 10 they have lost the pin, but if you are very lucky you will find one intact with the pin, and possibly even with some decorative enamel like that shown above right. There are various sub groups of these brooches, which we will not worry about here!

Other Roman brooches are zoomorphic (made to look like an animal). Here is a chicken brooch and a beautifully stylised horse's head brooch, but hares (not rabbits - they were introduced by the Normans!), birds and fish are common. Remember that they would originally have been a radiant polished copper colour and not the green we see today!

Three animal brooches: cockerel (left), horse's head (right), and hare (below).

Other Roman brooches are different again. The onebelow right looks to all the world like a piece of Victorian costume jewellery, but it's not; so be careful what you throw away, particularly if you are new to the hobby! Indeed the variety of Roman brooches is remarkable. Some are quite phallic, and they did seem to have a thing about a winged penis but, as this is a family book, I have shied away from illustrating that!

Roman plate brooch with glass stone.

More respectable are enamelled disc brooches and others that can be in the shape of surprising objects such as a shoe, a knife, or almost anything! As with most things Roman, brooches were produced on a large scale, certainly by the standards of the ancient world and traded both locally and across the Empire; there is even evidence to suggest that broken brooches were recycled!

An enamelled disc brooch is shown that must have looked quite beautiful when new, and a "shoe" brooch with traces of the enamelling left within.

Roman umbonate brooch (left), and shoe or sandal brooch.

Roman penannular brooch.

Roman mount - although the "wig" looks 18th century.

Brooches in the form of a ring can be found in any period. If the ring is complete they are called annular and, if there is a small gap, penannular. Decorated annular brooches, particularly silver ones, may well be medieval but rather plain; copper alloy (or even silver) penannular ones are most likely Roman. They have marked terminals and a simple pin that is larger than the diameter.

A mount is anything that fixes onto an object instead of a person and, given their love of "things", it follows that Roman mounts also crop up, and in many forms. I will show just one, a quite wonderful furniture mount found by a club member.

I am embarrassed to admit that when I first saw this object I tried to convince the finder that it was Georgian. "Look at the hairstyle!" I cried. Well I feel a fool now, but the moral of the story is that the more objects you handle the better at identification you get, and be very cautious when making statements about unusual items!

Anything Anglo-Saxon (still more so if Viking) is a rare find indeed. Some early Saxon brooches show a direct evolution from late Roman ones, although they soon developed their own style and begin to look quite different. Anything with swirly patterns or with abstract intertwining "beasties" should raise your suspicions, but don't get too excited too soon!

Saxon saucer brooch.

However, just to show that Saxon things do occasionally appear, here are a couple to look at. That on the right is a variation on a disc with a raised rim and is called, sensibly, a saucer brooch. It is early Saxon, 5th or 6th century, and may well have been originally gilded. They are predominantly found in central Southern England.

Saxon stirrup mount.

At the other end of the Saxon period is this, rather haunting, 11th century stirrup mount in the form of a human mask. These too seem to crop up in the area of "Wessex". This one appears to have been reused as a pendant.

In the medieval period most sorts of decoration seemed to focus on the power of the aristocracy or the church - those who fought or those who prayed. Hence mounts and pendants are often either heraldic or ecclesiastical in nature. The following example is a pilgrim mount, perhaps of 13th or 14th century date, and this might have been bought at a site of pilgrimage, perhaps Canterbury (St Thomas a Beckett) or Durham (St Cuthbert). Such places seemed to have done a roaring trade in religious "souvenirs", which might include a pilgrim badge or a small lead bottle of holy water (an ampulla) kept securely around your neck with a light chain for your return journey.

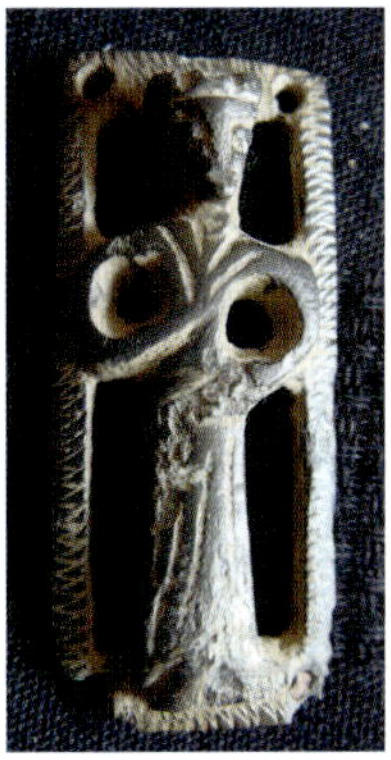

A 13th century pilgrim mount.

The heraldic shield, on the bottom right, is a horse harness pendant. It has a suspension loop at the top and the remains of once very fine enamelling; in this case it shows the three lions of England, the royal crest. It would have been one of several hanging from a knightly horse and purely decorative in nature; they are not unusual finds (image courtesy of the PAS). However, to find one in excellent condition is very rare and, I imagine, rather exciting. I actually found one of these myself but the condition of it is so embarrassingly poor that I couldn't bring myself to include a picture.

Medieval horse harness pendant.

Shown on the right is a rather fancy medieval annular brooch (image courtesy of the PAS) with an intact pin. This one has coloured glass stones in mounts around the rim although some have fallen out. Others of this type have decorated silver rims.

Medieval brooch.

Buckles & Strap Ends

You will find buckles - lots of buckles! It is easy to look down on them as being humdrum objects of everyday life but metal detecting is mostly about that; only rarely do we find real treasure! So we ought to know a little about the buckles we find as that makes our day a little more interesting. In the Iron Age, you (very occasionally) come across things called terret rings - beautiful objects used for horse harnesses. Roman buckles are often zoomorphic, meaning they take the shapes of animals.

A typical Roman design is to have the heads of animals, usually "dolphins" or horses, facing each other at the end of the loop.

Roman buckle.

Superb Viking buckle.

Next, we take a quick look at a superb Viking buckle (right). The design is intricate and complex; and, if you look hard enough, you can spot intertwining creatures in such forms. I had to include this image as it is such a wonderful object; however, let's come down to earth and look at more common finds!

All of the above are rare and so - before we get carried away with Celtic chariots - let's focus on what you are likely to find in your field! Buckles have different styles and, to a point, these did come in and out of fashion. But the design of a medieval buckle might not be that different from the one you may have on your belt as you read this; after all they are primarily functional. So the best we can do is illustrate a small but typical selection with descriptions and some rough dates. If you want to know more then I recommend the book by Ross Whitehead (see the "Further Reading" section).

Plain medieval buckle c.1400.

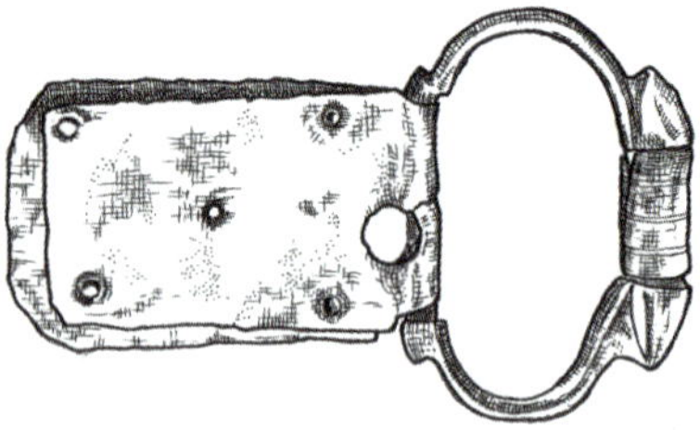

First (above) we have a typical medieval example. This is a single-looped buckle with attached plate and a roller bar on the loop. The pin has been lost (sadly) but some of the studs are intact as is the leather inside the plate (honest!). Of course, you might just find the plate or loop separately. Dating is hard but this buckle is probably late 13th to early 15th century.

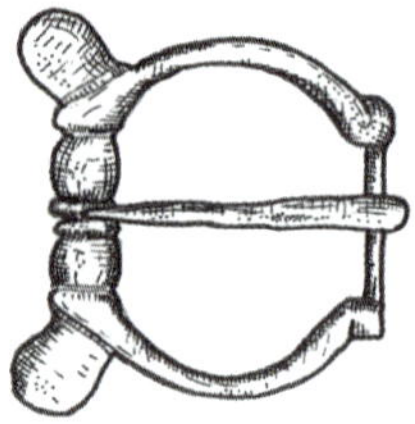

A single-looped medieval buckle is shown right, this time with the pin, and with two clearly protruding knobs. It was probably made in the late 13th to late 14th century. One of the giveaways is the imperfect casting of the pre-industrial age; the later buckles below are just a little too perfect!

On the right is an annular (circular) buckle. As always, this is hard to date with any precision but is probably a little later than the two above, at anywhere from the late 14th to 16th centuries.

The degree of decoration found in medieval buckles varies enormously. At one end they can be quite plain and functional. Then a little rustic decoration creeps in; and finally, for those who had the money to pay, there were beautifully made exquisite objects of solid silver or with gilding. See Benet's for some examples of the latter, but remember they are far from common finds!

These three little buckles are again cast copper alloy and are typical of the sort of thing you might find. The simple designs might suggest they are of an early date, but you really can't be sure. The left one is called a spectacle buckle and the right one a rectangular buckle. They were probably made in the 15th century but could be as late as the early 1700s.

Two rather plain medieval buckles.

The third (lower left) is a trapezoidal buckle. As for their use, that too is hard to say. They may have been part of clothing but, on farmland, may equally have been used for leather straps for horse tackle. The interpretation of buckles can be a frustrating business!

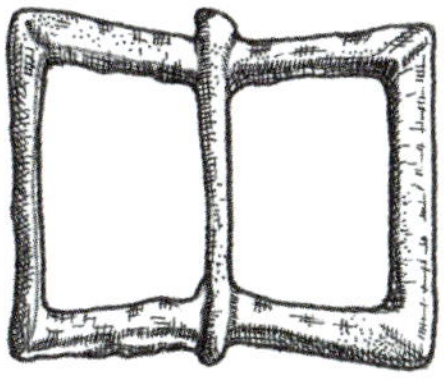

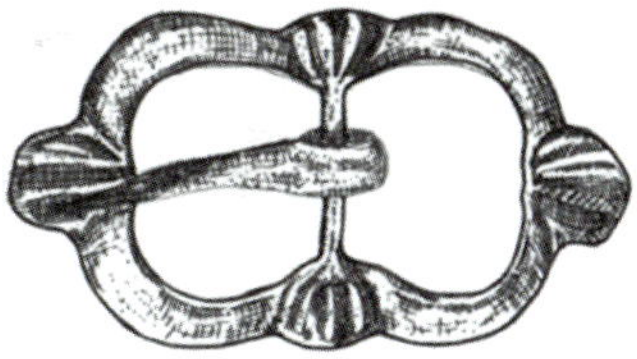

Three later buckles with a little more style.

As we get towards the 17th and 18th centuries identification gets a little easier as decoration becomes more commonplace. Compare the buckle above on the green background, from the 1600s, with the three mentioned above. It is a double loop asymmetrical buckle and, although it can hardly be described as ornate, there is a slight sense of fashion here and that, perhaps, reflects changes in society. The Middle Ages were gone and the middle class, with that extra disposable income, was on the rise. To continue the theme, here (right) is another spectacle buckle, but this is also from the 1600s and you can see the same modest decoration creeping in. The object is also a good reminder of how the iron, of the pin, corrodes far more rapidly than the copper alloy of the buckle.

Finally here is a shoe buckle I found lying on top of a ploughed field. From the 18th century, you can see that the style of the object has become as important as the function. The crossbar and pin are missing and the outer frame is broken but, even so, the decoration is clearly visible throughout; indeed people mistake it for a small picture frame!

18th century shoe buckle.

If buckles are a common find then strap ends are not. As the name suggests they are simply ornate metal endpoints for leather straps, popular in the Saxon and medieval periods. Here we have two Saxon strap ends. The first shows wonderful interweaving scrollwork beloved by Saxon craftsmen. This rare object would be a terrific find for even the most experienced detectorist. The second is zoomorphic, another Saxon theme, and looks like a dragon with a long neck and haunting eyes!

Two Saxon strap ends.

Buttons

When out detecting we all dream of hammered gold or a beautifully enamelled Roman brooch - well I do at least. The reality can often be a succession of shotgun cartridges or veterinary mastitis tubes On the scale of desirable finds buttons sit just on the border between rubbish and "mild interest" but rest assured you will find many, many buttons so you might as well make the most of them! Before the age of plastic, buttons were all metal and they apparently fell off clothing constantly! It's no surprise that we also find lots of thimbles in fields - evidence of on the spot repairs!

Yet, before you throw your buttons straight into the recycling, pause and have a good look at the humble objects as some really are mildly interesting and, in fact, can be worth more to collectors than the average silver hammered coin.

Personally, I am rather fond of "livery buttons", which were worn as a sort of uniform identifying the particular member of the landed gentry for whom you worked. The designs are based on heraldic images and often sit on a straight piece of twisted rope; sometimes it is possible, with a bit of research, to identify the aristocratic family from the emblem. Unfortunately, as they are less than 300 years old (probably late 18th or early 19th century), you might have to do the research yourself unless you can charm your FLO into making an exception and doing it for you.

Because I live on Salisbury Plain I accumulate a fair few military buttons, and there is a new book to be written on that subject alone (though not by us). The earlier infantry buttons have the regimental number written clearly upon them and, if you wish, you could then find out a little of the regimental history. So, for example, the button on the right is the 66th Regiment of Foot.

Later buttons were of a more standardised "royal crest" design.

How old is my button? Your starting point, as with most objects, is the quality of manufacture. If it is machine made it will look perfectly round, probably with stamped writing on the back, and the attachment loop will be perfectly centred. If it all looks a little "rough and ready" it was probably made locally before the Industrial Revolution. If so, you may find the design on the front is also a bit hit and miss. Buttons of this period may have floral designs, weave patterns (see right) or simply a geometrical shape.

Livery buttons - common but interesting finds.

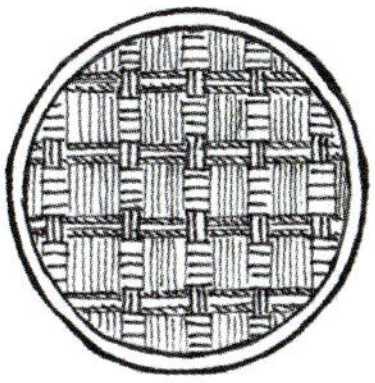

Some buttons will remain a bit of a mystery. The example on the right has the Prince of Wales emblem and the initials HH. No doubt somebody will know what this means but I don't - so please feel free to enlighten me!

Many 19th century buttons have the maker's name on the back. As well as adding a little interest, this can be used to try and date the button, as manufacturers came in and out of business. Records may not be complete but the information is often out there, and for anything local your nearby museum should be able to help; yet another reason to be nice to your FLO.

To make the point, this rather nice livery button, with some remaining gilding, was made by "Stevens, Blackmore & Sons" of Salisbury. I confess that I have not followed this up, but I will - promise!

A local Salisbury livery button.

Even 20th century buttons can tell you something. Those with four central eyelets ("braces" buttons) sometimes have the manufacturer on the front and its origins will, quite often, be local. Saxon gold it is not, but at least it keeps the brain ticking! The one shown was made by "J. Noyes" of Pewsey in Wiltshire, which is just up the road from where I live.

Buttons were used (and lost) back to the medieval period (and before); but these are rare and not at all straightforward to identify. If you are interested in these things I would direct you to Brian Read's definitive guide (see "Further Reading"). However, just to show that the topic is not all 18th and 19th century, I include one very early example of a button and loop fastener, which is one of my favourite finds.

These were used (probably) to act as a fastener for a cloak and made just before, and after, the Roman invasion, so date 1st century. There are variations on a theme, some looking a little like duffle coat fasteners, but this is one of which I am very fond. Note the "eye" design. It is hard not to think that this little object was functional and aesthetic, but also spiritual insofar as it kept away bad spirits for the vulnerable traveller. Objects can tell you so much!

Celtic or Roman loop fastener.

Rings

Finger rings have been popular for 2,000 years. They are easily lost and, unsurprisingly, crop up every so often when metal detecting. Of those that come your way most will be modern, but potentially still interesting, and if beach detecting is your thing then you will find such rings quite regularly. Cold sea water makes fingers shrink and off slips the wedding ring. Snow has the same effect and I have been called out, in a blizzard, to help a damsel in distress find both her wedding and engagement rings. We found them, much to her delight! Gardening also takes its toll, and rings fall off when gloves are being removed. Of course, rings and fingers have been parting company throughout history and so, now and then, you might dig up a finger ring that is not at all modern.

The Romans loved all sorts of what we might now call "bling", and finger rings were popular. It is dangerous to talk of a standard design as these rings come in many different forms but there is a common profile that is easily recognised. They can appear quite chunky, with a rounded shape and, at the front, can become quite wide with a broad, elliptical stone inserted. Often this intaglio may have a figure carved in it, which may have been used as a form of signet ring (see *Benet's Artefacts* - 2nd Ed pp177-195). Unlike medieval rings, they don't often carry "modern" precious gems. The bronze example, right, has a missing intaglio but nicely shows the typical Roman shape.

Roman ring minus its stone.

Mind you, some Roman rings seem to be more than decorative. For years rings with the inscription "ToT" have been turning up in Lincolnshire and the FLO there, a very

nice chap called Adam Daubney, has been making a study of them. The map shows their distribution, or at least it did until my detecting partner Nick Barrett found this one in Wiltshire! Anyway, Adam believes them to be a sort of devotional ring to a Celtic god "Totatis" worshipped by the Corieltauvi tribe in, what is now called, Lincolnshire. In 2001 only nine rings of this type were known but, thanks to metal detectorists, no less than 66 have now been recorded with the PAS and they are providing invaluable data for his research.

Roman ToT ring.

What You Can Find - Artefacts

Roman bronze snake ring.

A rather different style of Roman ring symbolises rebirth and healing. The snake ring can be made of gold and be a high status item; however, this rather more humble example is made of copper alloy.

Saxon and Viking rings do exist and perhaps you will be lucky enough to find one - but it's not likely so let's move on to the medieval period!

Any medieval, or Tudor, ring is a wonderful find. Signet rings, for example, with a carved initial, allow you that personal connection with the original anonymous owner and you can imagine them being used to add a personal seal to wax. They are quite big and masculine looking as are iconographic rings (i.e. those with religious images, presumably worn by members of the clergy or by monks). But, for the most part, medieval rings are more delicate in appearance. Indeed, were it not for the obvious "handmade" quality about them, they look much like modern rings made for the female hand. They may also contain precious stones.

Fede rings have a clasped hands motif. Their use was quite common throughout the later medieval period and into the 16th century (and I believe, even today). They were romantic in nature and vary from ornate gold or silver examples to rustic pewter forms.

Medieval Fede ring.

On the right is an early 16th century example from the rustic tradition. Made of debased silver, I found it shortly after starting the hobby. I remember that the landowner, a good friend of mine, described it as "something out of a Christmas cracker"!

Posy ring with inscription.

In the post medieval period mourning rings became popular. They are perhaps a little morbid to our taste as they were made after a person's death and worn as a form of remembrance; indeed provision was often made in the will for their manufacture and distribution! They are usually inscribed on the outside with the initials of the deceased and even a date of death. They may have a black decoration.

On a more cheerful note are posy rings, which are plain gold bands with a little romantic rhyme (the posy) engraved on the inside so it would only be known to the married couple (or lovers). Each year a handful of these go through the Treasure process and (remarkably) in 2007 I found one! The posy on mine reads "The Love is True that I O.U. x"; perhaps a little sickly by today's standards but there you have it. It was dated to the end of the 17th century and so (just) came into the Treasure category of over 300 years. As it is the only gold thing I have ever found I thought it deserved a picture!

Seals

Seal matrices showing inscriptions.

Some detectorists prefer to find coins over artefacts, but artefacts are more personal and there can be few objects that connect you with the original owner more personally than seal matrices. Medieval matrices (the word "seal" can refer to either the matrix or the wax imprint) were used in a time where signatures were not common in a broadly illiterate age. The seals of royalty and the nobility were attached to ribbons hanging from the bottom of documents and were rather large. For everyone else, matrices were between 1-2cm in diameter and, depending on your importance (and probably budget), made of silver, bronze or lead (like that above).

Seal matrix showing top, base and a wax impression.

The better off had bespoke matrices, with an abbreviation of their name in Latin or French; those for more humble folk were generic and "off the shelf". Like so many objects we find, these seals have gone from being rarities in museums to relatively collectable items - all thanks to the numbers found, and recorded, by metal detectorists. If you are lucky enough to find one of these then you are advised, by professional conservators, *not* to take a wax impression as the wax can remove small fragments of a fragile matrix. However, as this lovely bronze example I found is in excellent condition, I ignored the advice and took one anyway. It is probably 14th century and has a "fleur de lys" emblem in the centre with the script around the edge reading, S. h DEPEChy. Chi, which means "seal of (sigillum) H. de Pechy of [possibly] Chippenham". To be able to link an object with a named individual who lived 600 years ago is quite magical! This example is quite unusual, in being hexagonal at the base, as most examples of this period are round, but is otherwise typical of matrices with suspension loops sitting atop a stem.

Vesica seal matrix.

Slightly earlier, perhaps late 13th century, is the pointed oval matrix (called a vesica shape). They are a different design in that the suspension loop is at the top of a strengthening ridge on the reverse of the matrix and so the whole thing is quite flat in appearance.

A gold fob seal and impression.

Fast forwarding to the 18th century, seals make a comeback, at least as finds. Georgian fob seals were highly fashionable for quite a long period. By this time the rise of the middle class had occurred and, unsurprisingly, these are much more common finds. Otherwise the parallels between these and their medieval counterparts are remarkable. Once again, at the top end of the market, they were highly decorative and made of solid gold or silver, but now had a separate centre piece, the intaglio, which had a bespoke family emblem or personal initials. Those of more humble stock had to be content with copper alloy and gilt with an intaglio which had an "off the shelf" design, just like their medieval forebears, often of some generic classical profile, like the one shown above.

Of course, you will never find a wax seal in the ground, but you might find an imprint in lead. The most dramatic of these are papal bullae, lead imprints of the seal of the Pope to be found on all documents sent out from Rome to medieval Catholic countries which, pre-Reformation, included England and Scotland. Molten lead was poured over a cord, hanging from the document, and the impression made.

Lead papal bulla.

Not quite such an impressive find, but still mildly interesting (especially as it was found on an otherwise miserable day), is the lead bag or bale seal, such as that shown on the right. This one is probably 19th century, although they can be older, and was probably used for bags of seeds or something similar.

Lead bale seal.

Tokens

Not every round piece of metal is a coin! Most such finds are, of course, buttons, but even after you dismiss those there is another category of artefacts: the humble token. These are "coin-like objects" that, if you are not careful can often fool you; but when you find one (and you will) do not be disheartened, for they are often really interesting!

Tokens, of one sort or another, have been around since the 14th century; but their appearance, scarcity and even function often changes. So let's take a quick look at what you might dig up.

Jettons

Sometimes called "reckoning counters", these were in use from the late medieval period through to the late 17th century. The early ones were made in England and then later, by the 15th century, often imported from France, many (not all) from the town of Tournai. They can be quite large, about the size of a pre decimal penny and often have French heraldic images. In good condition they can be quite beautiful although not particularly valuable Here is an elegant example dating from the late 15th century.

French jetton from Tournai.

By the 16th century the Germans seem to have cornered the market, and vast numbers were exported, from Nuremburg in particular. These are a little smaller and often have an "orb and cross" motif on one side. The German text will often tell you the maker although, on the reverse side, most have some fairly meaningless saying.

This one was found in the front garden of an old mill, just the place where you would expect the trading of goods to be going on. It was made by Hans Krauwinckel in the late 16th century.

A later German jetton.

So what were jettons used for during all this time? Well, the standard answer is that they have no face value, but instead were used by traders to do calculations. In an age without pencil or paper, a cloth would be produced with drawn horizontal lines, a bit like an abacus. A jetton, placed upon a certain line, would have a certain "value". By moving them around, a trader could do all the sums necessary to work out a bill or to work out the change: all very clever!

Usually they are found singly but, on a club day out some years ago, Stuart Bailey and Nigel Wright found a jetton hoard outside

Jetton hoard found by Stuart Bailey and Nigel Wright.

the entrance to a medieval church. Apparently it was not unusual for trading to take place just beyond consecrated ground! Details of the hoard can be found in the PAS report for 2005/6 (page 90).

So many jettons are found in all manner of sites that some archaeologists speculate that perhaps they were, at least for periods, used as "small change" and it is entirely possible that over the centuries that they were in circulation that their practical use did alter. Some research is needed here.

Lead Tokens

Usually small and roughly made these quite distinctive objects are a bit of a mystery. The consensus is that they are late medieval (but that could easily stretch to the 17th century) and they might have been used as small change in a local market. But no one really knows. These objects were clearly used by the common folk and the details of their lives were never well documented. Certain designs crop up regularly, such as the weave or the anchor, and there may be regional variation. Personally I think they are lovely objects and make a great find.

Lead tokens made locally.

17th Century Trade Tokens

Thankfully we know a little more about these! They were produced by local tradesmen as a response to a desperate shortage of low value coinage. They appeared for a brief period from the 1640s until the Crown started issuing official copper coinage in 1672. In my (limited) experience most seem to date from the 1660s and are usually quite small, the size of a modern 1p piece, and have a face value of a farthing (¼d). The recording of these tokens, with the PAS, provides invaluable information about the geographical spread of trade at that time. Many of them have the merchant's initials on them, as with the example on the right (in order: I, R, and surname V), along with the town of use (here, Colchester). A museum will often be able to identify these for you and you might even be able to find something interesting about the specific tradesman.

Late 18th Century Tokens

Another crisis resulting from a lack of small change occurred in the reign of George III. The Crown stopped minting copper coins in 1775 and soon they were in short supply. The situation was made far worse by the coming of the Industrial Revolution and the consequent migration of people from rural villages to industrial towns. Workers needed to be paid and coinage was sparse. Eventually in 1787, a copper mining company in Anglesey took matters into their own hands and started minting tokens. Quite soon, others copied this idea and by the early 1790s there were so many different designs that, even at the time, they became collectors' items!

Fairly common detecting finds, they are generally bigger (½d size) than their 17th century cousins and, being machine made, look much more "modern" in quality. They often have elegant designs and were distributed over wide areas - not just locally. The druid image (right) is perhaps the best known of these tokens and was a symbol of the Celtic heritage of Anglesey, home of the Parys mine. Other tokens take images from the classical world and some even

Anglesey token.

have advertising. Once again, in time, the government acted and there was a recoinage in 1797 when the famous "cartwheel" pennies were minted. Tokens were yet again banned; even so, many of them appear worn when dug out of the ground and must have remained in circulation for years after.

Weights

Today, if you buy a bag of flour, you assume that the weight on the packet is what you get; but it was not always so! A set of weights was essential if you were a trader dealing in loose produce and, because your customer probably thinks you're trying to pull a fast one, he will want to see an official stamp on your weight to confirm it is the weight it states. In return, the trader might want to check the weight of your coin to make sure you weren't trying to pass off some counterfeit or clipped coin. So here are a few examples that we have found.

Steelyard Weight

A steelyard was a portable device that allowed the trader to move weights along a bar and get them to act as counterweights for whatever was being measured. The Romans used them all the time, but they proved so useful that they remained in use right through the medieval period and well beyond.

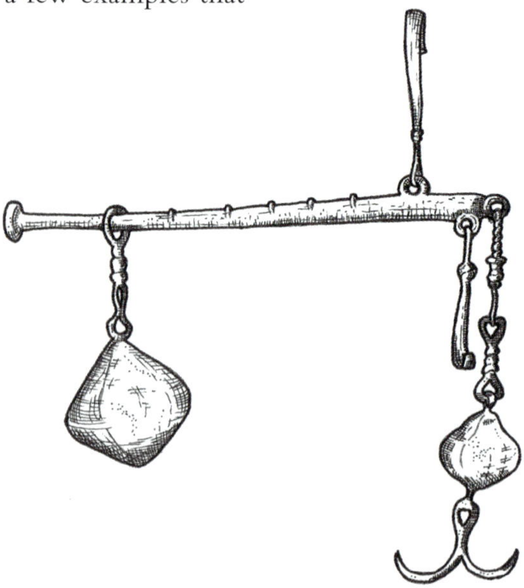

This is Micky's sketch of a Roman steelyard which is on display in the British Museum. You can see how it would have been suspended by the hook on the top, and the "claw" on the bottom right would have had a pan hanging down from it. The weight on the left is moveable so as to counterbalance whatever was in the pan.

The example shown on right is one of several found on a particular Roman site. It is a crude lump of lead, with a slightly "pear-shaped" profile with an iron attaching loop (broken) on the top. It is over 4cm long and piles in at a hefty 125g or so.

Roman crude lead steelyard weight.

They do come in different sizes. A detecting partner of mine Nick Barrett and I have found a complete set of these on the

Lead weights of various sizes and shapes.

site (shown above), and if ever you wanted evidence of trading at a particular location then this is surely it! It just goes to show that even an ugly lump of lead can give you a valuable insight into the past. Interestingly the 125g weight is the second lightest of the set, so they were weighing out substantial amounts! Not all Roman weights were as simply made, and they can be quite sophisticated in shape. If you are very lucky you may find one in the shape of a human, divine (god/goddess) or even an animal bust.

Medieval steelyard weights also vary considerably. On right is (I'm pretty sure) a medieval steelyard weight, although I wouldn't begin to give it a more precise date. It has a lead suspension loop and the base has been made into an angular shape - all very different from its Roman ancestor. The downmarket ones are still better made than the crude Roman lump and the upmarket ones can have heraldic emblems on them - like that illustrated right - and might well have been made of bronze. Of course, you might always unearth the steelyard itself - but that would be a fantastic find!

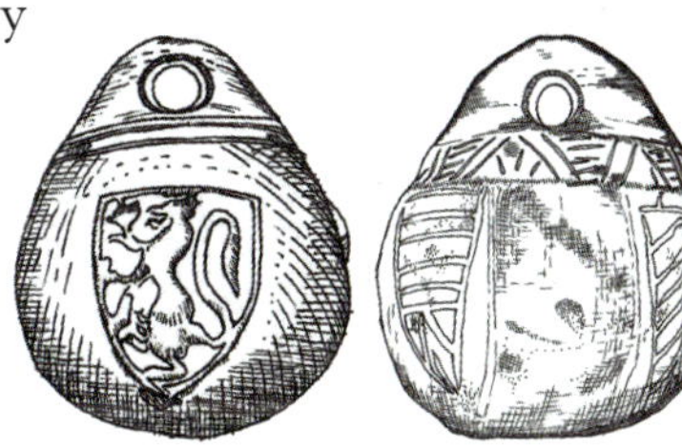

Trade Weights

Trade weights served a similar function to the steelyard weight. These were used on simple sets of scales and, as they had to lie flat and not hung, they are a very different shape.

Bronze 18th century trade weight.

Post medieval (18th century) trade weights are typically round and flat with the earlier ones made of lead (often hard to date as they have no markings). By and large, the later ones are of brass. This one has stamps all over the place and seems to have been, unhelpfully, over-stamped with a ¼lb mark. Often the stamps are clearer and they can tell you quite a lot. The monarch might well be shown as a crown with an abbreviation beneath; so a crown with VR or GIII would show Victoria or George III. This was important as it meant that the accuracy of the weight was backed by the authority of the state and you messed with that at your peril!

Another common mark is a large A, which stands for "Avoirdupois". In the medieval period there were, confusingly, two systems of weight in operation: Troy ounces and Avoirdupois ounces, and these differed from each other. Over time Troy ounces went out of use (apart from with precious metals where they are still used today) and a local market would only see Avoirdupois trade weights. Some weights also show "hallmarks" and one of the most common is a sword, indicating London. For anything else - enjoy your research!

Lead trade weight.

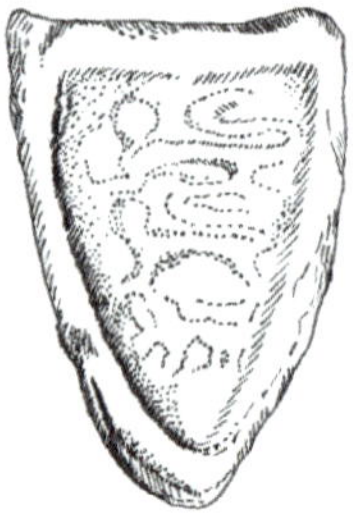

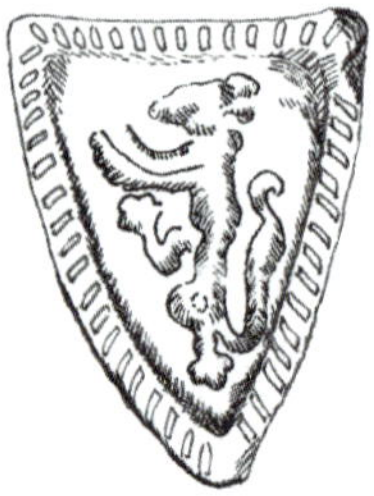

Some earlier medieval trade weights were not circular but often made into rather crude shields with heraldic images (illustrated right). They often have holes in them presumably to string them together.

Coin Weights

On the right are two photographs of a coin weight of James I. These are often (not always!) square and are made to match the exact weight of a particular gold coin. The value of that coin might be found on the obverse and a similar image to that found on the coin itself, might be found on the reverse - useful when such coins were so rare.

Coin weight of James I.

This one is for a gold coin called a "unite", worth 22 (XXII) shillings. You can just about make out the king, with orb and sceptre on the reverse which matches the real coin.

The whole point was to discourage counterfeiting of coins and also the "clipping" of the edges of hammered coins. A merchant would have a boxed set of coin weights and use them to check the weight of high value coins offered to him in trade. Throughout the medieval and post medieval periods foreign coins would be circulating and so you come across weights for these too, or at least the high value ones. Many of these were made in Antwerp, and always carry a motif of a flat hand.

This Antwerp weight, found in Wiltshire, was designed to counterbalance a Hungarian ducat (hence "HD"). European trade is nothing new and by recording finds such as these, with the PAS, you will add to our understanding of how that trade worked.

Antwerp coin weight.

Loom Weights & Spindle Whorls

A spindle whorl is a plain, ringed doughnut-shaped lead object used for teasing out the fibres of wool to make yarn. Sometimes they are decorated with dots and triangles but more often not. They were used to create the tension to allow the yarn to wrap around the "drop" spindle. Now I know you didn't take up the hobby of metal detecting to learn about textile manufacture but I include this little diagram of how it's supposed to work for your self improvement.

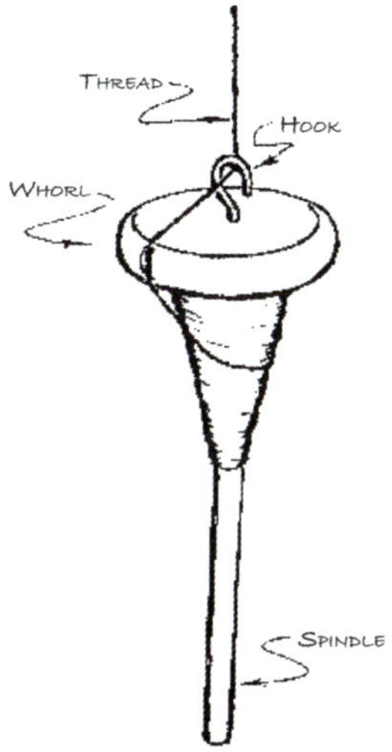

Then there are loom weights, a term often, wrongly, interchanged with spindle whorl. These were used, in a certain type of vertical loom, and in the illustration below, drawn by Dianne Leahy and kindly provided by her and Kevin Leahy, you can see the weights hanging down at the bottom to pull down various yarns in the weaving process. It is likely that most of these were quite a bit bigger than the spindle whorls but, to be honest, I think they used any old lump of lead, stone or ceramic around so the shape may not be an accurate guide to their use.

Lead loom weight.

What You Can Find - Artefacts

"Prehistoric" Artefacts

What we mean by "prehistoric" is the time before written records and before history, and for us in Britain that means pre-Roman. Archaeologists break the term down further into different "ages", depending on what materials were being used at the time, and it is worth having a look at this if, for no other reason, than we will know what the experts are talking about!

Palaeolithic	500,000-12,000 BC	Ice Ages, mammoths!
Mesolithic	2,000-4,000 BC	Hunter-gatherers in forests
Neolithic	4,000-2 000 BC	Farming!
Bronze Age	2,000-800 BC	Bronze axes, spears
Iron Age	800 BC-AD 43	Coins, trade with Rome

Palaeolithic (meaning "old stone age") refers to the period since the arrival of human species to Europe and the vast ocean of time when they survived the ebbs and flows of various Ice Ages. For most of this period, from about 500,000 years ago, these were not even modern humans but our evolutionary cousins, the Neanderthals. We, Homo Sapiens, evolved in Africa about 200,000 years ago and there we stayed, geographically trapped, until a few hundred individuals (yes, all non-Africans on the entire planet are descended from this small group) managed to migrate perhaps 80,000 years ago. "We" arrived in Northern Europe only about 45,000 years ago bringing our stone tools, art, and way of life; hunting and utilising herds of wild animals in the cold environment. There is no pottery, no metal artefacts, and evidence of any kind is rare indeed. You will not find any!

With the retreat of the glaciers, about 12,000 years ago, and the rise of the sea level, Britain and Ireland slowly began to become separate from the European mainland and become islands. They were forested and the people were "hunter gatherers". They were transient, hunted deer and game, but also relied on plants and increasingly had temporary seasonal bases to which they might return year on year. This was the Mesolithic era ("middle stone age"), and the entire population of Britain may have been merely a couple of thousand people or so - you might rarely encounter anybody outside your extended family! That is quite a thought, and the whole subject is fascinating, but still not of any direct relevance to a metal detectorist!

In our hobby we should start to pay attention in the Neolithic ("new stone age"). This is when the idea of farming arrived at our shores about 4000 BC (about 6,000 years ago) having spread from, what is now, Iran. Farming changed everything. People now stayed with their crops and were no longer always on the move. Surplus food could be grown and populations increase. Innovation could occur, like pottery, and society could support specialists like priests. This was when monuments started to be built: long barrows, early stone circles, and the like. Apart from the rare bit of gold there is still no metal, but the use of flint became prolific. Eyes only finds are inevitable when, as a detectorist, you spend hours staring at the ground, and it is well worth learning to recognise the distinctive design of Neolithic pottery and even the signs of worked flint.

Neolithic axe head (eyes only find).

This is a Neolithic flint axe head I found just lying on the surface. It may be a bit battered, but it is about 5,000 years old and just shows why you should never detect too fast! Very occasionally highly polished ceremonial axe heads are found from this period.

Neolithic pottery looks pretty crude to the modern eye. It was used for domestic storage, and was thick with rounded bottoms and sometimes decorated with bits of cord or with dots around the rim. The potters' wheel had yet to be invented so it was made by coiling a long "sausage" of clay and then firing the pot on an open fire, which supplied a fairly low temperature. Such pots must have broken very easily.

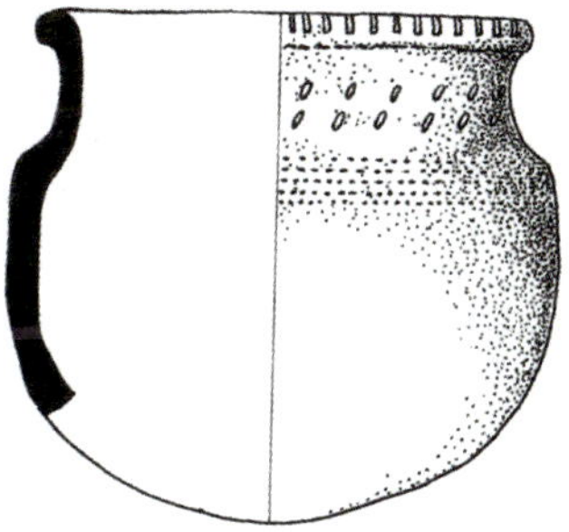

Bronze is an alloy of copper with a little tin. The tin strengthens the metal crystal making it much more hard wearing and much more useful than copper alone. Most of Europe started with a "Copper Age" and only later moved to bronze but, thanks to all that accessible Cornish tin, we bypassed that and the Bronze Age started in Britain about 2,000 BC. The thing is that at the same time, everything else changed too. The elite were now buried, with grave goods, in round barrows; pottery became more sophisticated, and the evidence is compelling that society became much more hierarchical and complex. Archaeologists argue heatedly about whether all this represents a migration of new people (sometimes called the "Beaker People") or simply a migration of new ideas coming from Europe. That debate is not for the likes of us but at last we can now find metal objects!

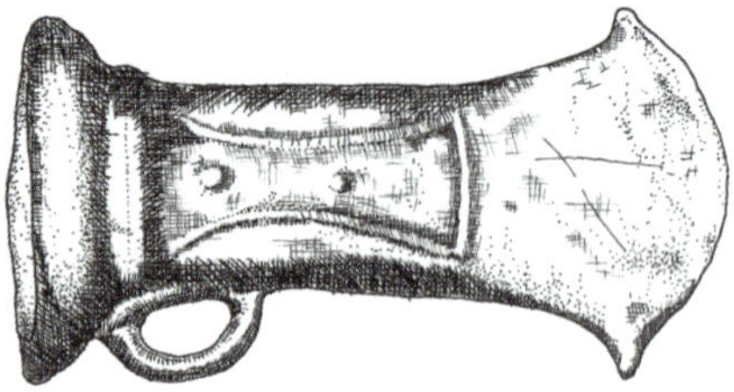

Bronze Age axe head.

Shown above is a beautiful middle Bronze Age palstave type axe head that Nick Barrett found sitting on the top of a field! A pound coin is shown for scale. Objects such as these, which required great skill to make, seemed to have a use beyond that of the merely practical and, in the later Bronze Age, became a sort of early currency - a way to store your wealth and display your status. The drawing above right shows the more common loop and socketed axe style and if you are really lucky you might even come across a socketed spearhead!

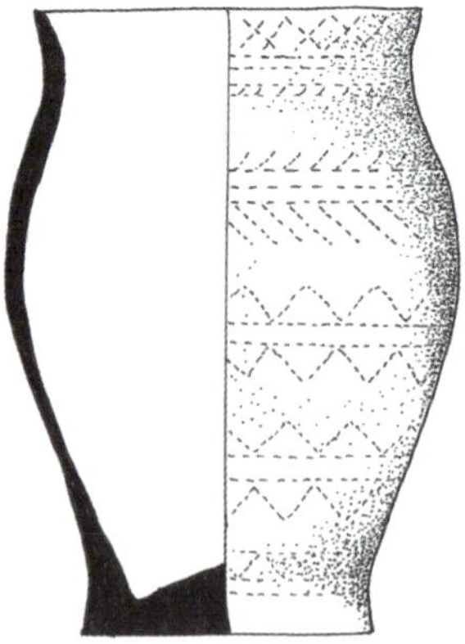

Bronze Age pottery is far more sophisticated than Neolithic. The iconic form is the "beaker", a tall, elegant, slightly-curved vessel with high decoration, a flat bottom and thin walls (see right). Always keep an eye out for an unusual decorated shard and, if you find one, record it with your FLO in the usual way.

In the late Bronze Age large hoards of axe heads and ingots, containing sometimes hundreds of items, often never used, are buried and hence discovered by detectorists. Why they were buried is a hot archaeological topic, but it could be a symptom of an economic collapse, perhaps caused by the discovery of a new "wonder" metal, iron.

The Iron Age arrived in Western Europe at about 800 BC. There is a much wider array of objects that you might stumble across with your detector and, although none are exactly common, they do turn up from time to time. Of course, bronze - being pretty and not susceptible to rusting - was still the preferred metal for decorative objects. In brooches and fasteners, sometimes with colourful glass enamel, can be seen a variety of stylised swirls and abstract patterns. Celtic art was very different from the realistic representation on later Roman objects.

The illustration (right) is of a strap junction, probably from a horse harness. Also, have a look at those Celtic coins, looked at earlier, to see what I mean. A guide like *Benet's Artefacts* is an excellent starting point to see what might be found!

Iron Age strap junction.

Miscellaneous

Bells

Oddly, I once went through a period of finding bicycle bells in the middle of fields. They were recovered on different farms on different days but there they were, being pulled out of the ground on a regular basis. I must have found half a dozen in as many months, and I haven't found any since (not that I'm upset). There is no pattern in what we find!

Nice example of a crotal bell.

More sensibly you may find crotal bells, small bells that hung from various farm animals such as sheep or shire horses. Or, I should say, at least in my neck of the woods you will find them, as in southern England they are quite common finds; but not for you Northerners and Scots. I presume it was a question of fashion, and I really don't know where the limit of these bells is to be found but there it is.

They appear in the early post medieval period, seem to reach their heyday in the 18th century, and then gradually fade away from history. They are spherical, with a suspension loop and two sound holes in the upper half with an iron ball inside. The bottom hemisphere, by the 18th century, was often decorated with a flowering petal design and sometimes had the maker's initials. With a little research, these makers can sometimes be identified. Finding one that still rings is always a pleasure, although fragments are more common.

Two marked crotal bells.

Of the two bells on the right, the (considerably) larger one has a clear "RW" on the bottom. This is "Robert Wells", who had a bell foundry in the Wiltshire village of Aldbourne in the 18th century. The smaller bell has "RN" as the maker and I have failed to identify this. If you know, please tell me!

Bells with an integrated suspension loop (i.e. where they have been cast out of the same piece of metal and the hole simply drilled through), are thought to be older than those which have a square frame attached. For that matter, if you dig up a bell decorated with fish then that is likely to be a 17th century example.

Earlier (left) and later example of crotal bells.

Pot Mends

Like most new to the hobby I had no idea at all what this odd lead thing was when I first dug one up. They are from a "lost age" when things of value were mended rather than replaced When a ceramic pot became damaged with a small hole in the bottom then the "mend" was to pour a little molten lead into the hole and allow it to solidify above and below. The now sealed hole would be fine until the pot eventually broke and was discarded. The pot mend would now look like a lead sandwich with, if you are lucky, a little ceramic left between. I've even got one with an imprint of the cloth upon which the pot was resting when it was fixed!

Pot mends - these could date anywhere from Roman to medieval.

Swords & Daggers

The Bronze Age apart, the blades of swords and daggers are made of steel and, even if they do survive rusting away in the ground, you will miss them if you are using discrimination on your detector. However, that is not true for the "accessories" and the bits and pieces associated with them vary in substance and style over the centuries.

Pommels are the tops of the "handle" and are pretty rare things. Well okay, that is unless you were the finder of the Staffordshire Hoard, which contained several dozen Saxon examples decorated with gold!

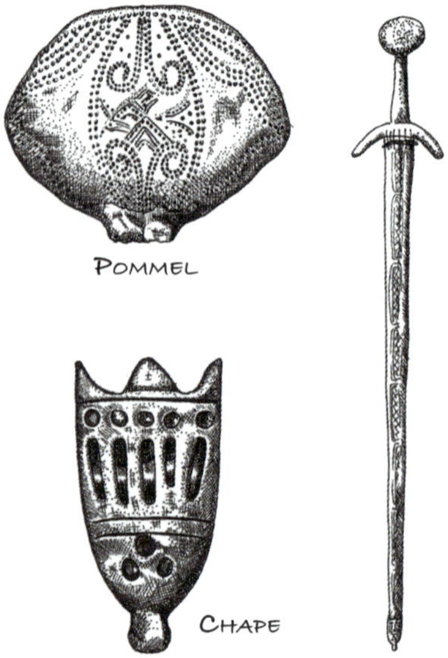

At the other end of the scabbard is the chape. Its job is to hold the point of the blade, and when the leather of the scabbard rots away then the chape may well be all that survives in the ground. As swords are larger than daggers, they can vary in size and in decoration, from the highly ornate to the plain, as shown here in the photograph. Its simplicity makes it hard to date, but it is likely to be late medieval or early post medieval. You can see a small hole (top right) where the leather would have been attached.

Plain sword chape.

A more likely find is a Tudor sword hanger, or at least part of one, like that on the right. This one is only half complete but the top bar would have been fastened to the belt, and the two (or often three) hangers would have fastened to the top of the scabbard. This would give lots of flexibility in movement for the sword. They are often decorated (oddly) with botanical designs.

Part of a Tudor sword belt hanger.

Thimbles

Until you start detecting you would have no idea how common thimbles are, of all ages, in our fields. I suppose it is a comment on the "make and mend" way of thinking of our forebears, and the stark reality of poverty, that you made instant repairs on your clothes when doing hard physical work. That said, some thimbles are clearly items of status.

The top one shown is called a "beehive" thimble. It could be between the 15th and 16th centuries in date and you can see how the dimples were all handmade and spiral out from the apex. I never thought I would ever get excited about a thimble but it really is a lovely thing. It seems there are a lot of thimble collectors out there, and examples in excellent condition are surprisingly valuable! The middle is a little later in date, probably 17th century, and is solid silver. The third, also silver, is later still, (19th century).

Thimbles: early (top) to Victorian (bottom).

Other Roman Artefacts

Roman society was sophisticated, hierarchical and survived on the wealth produced by trade. Consumer goods were produced in enormous quantities, both locally and throughout the Empire and the desire to own "stuff" was much more like our own world than the early medieval period that followed. So the variety of Roman artefacts that can be found is wide and fascinating. As always I cannot be exhaustive but it is worth looking at a few, fairly random, examples of what might just turn up.

What You Can Find - Artefacts

Here is a piece of Roman armour. Well, I say that as it was originally identified as such but it is, apparently, an object without parallel and now our FLO thinks it may be Saxon! In any event, it is rectangular with two suspension loops at the top, and an attachment lug at the back. I have told the club member who found this that I think it is the most beautiful metal detecting artefact I have ever seen! The cartoon face is utterly modern and has an expression that is hard to pin down but reminds me a little of the expressions on the Lewis chessmen in the British Museum. I absolutely love it!

The Romans produced all sorts of little instruments made for specific purposes. Some of these were medical and others were cosmetic in nature. A Roman gentleman might carry a metal ring to which would be attached several of these things, including, perhaps, some tweezers, a toothpick, ear scoop, and even a device for smartening up your nail cuticles (can't say I have one of these myself), like that shown. It is about 10cm long, is of twisted copper-alloy wire and is very hard to photograph properly! One end has an attachment loop and the other is flattened out.

Some more experienced detectorists will complain that there is no separate section on keys. Well there isn't, but as a peace offering here is a 14cm long Roman example. Perhaps this object, more than any other, represents the modernity that the Romans brought to these islands.

Spirituality was central to all aspects of Roman life. A wide range of gods were seen to intervene directly and regularly on a daily basis and so many finds relate to this. This is a stunning example of a statuette (this is about 6cm high), which would probably have been carried around and used as a focus to prayer. On a related note, you might come across Roman objects that seem to have been deliberately been broken and put beyond use.

Roman armour (?).

Roman cosmetic implements.

Roman key.

Small Roman statuette.

These are called votive offerings, and another example is this lovely miniature cauldron found by Nick Barrett. Also found by Nick is a rather fine Roman decorative pin.

Small votive offering.

Roman pin.

Roman Pottery

This is not a book on ceramics, but we ought to say just a little about Roman pottery as, if you start to find Roman metal objects, you will undoubtedly come across shards aplenty! For those of you who want to learn more about this I would direct you to the Further Reading secton at the back of the book.

The most "posh" form, and the easiest to recognise, is called samian ware.This was used for tableware and has a distinctive and rich iron red colour, with a shiny surface finish. It was produced, mainly in Gaul, in huge quantities and exported to wealthy homes across the Empire. Some examples were highly decorated, although many were relatively plain. If you are lucky you might find a maker's stamp on the base. The piece on the left has DVPIVSF and the final F stands for fecit (made); so, in effect, "made by Dupius".

Two pieces of samian ware.

Amphorae, by contrast, were huge thick storage containers that may have contained wine, oil or anything imported into provincial Britain. Below are some complete ones, in the British Museum, and a broken handle piece, which is more the sort of thing that you might find!

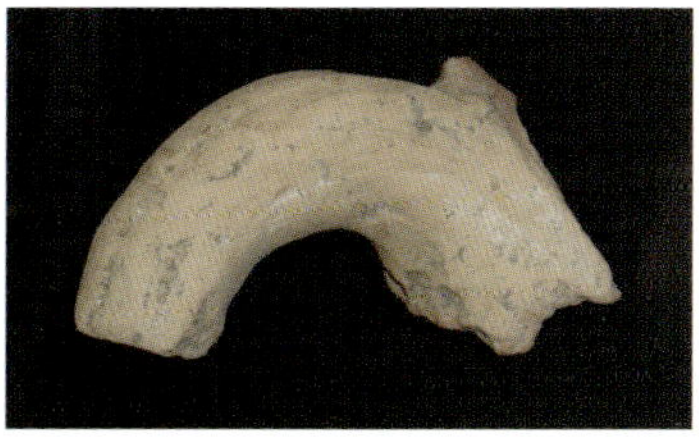

Broken off amphora handle found in a field.

Roman amphorae in the British Museum.

Kitchenware, at least in Britain, is dominated by, what is called, black burnished ware, which can be black or grey and quite be quite dumpy in appearance.

Mosaic floors were a luxury that only the well-off Romans or Romanised Celtic leaders could afford.

Single tesserae.

Single pieces of tesserae were hand cut from different types of stone and pottery, roughly cubic in shape, so that Roman artisans could make patterns from the different colours to create a fantastic patterned picture on the floor of a villa. These tesserae are usually found near the site of a Roman building or, just perhaps, where a bag has split that was being transported to a building site.

Mosaic floor made from tesserae.

Here, on the right, is a typical example of a mosaic showing part of a rope pattern encircling a series of flowers. The use of solitary tessera can be clearly seen to make up the desired shapes. Each piece was set in cement to form the pattern to a laid out plan. One square foot of flooring takes about 140-150 tesserae, so a room 15 by 20 feet big would take 40,000-45,000 pieces; and this is based on quite a large cube. If it was set with smaller pieces, to give a more detailed appearance, this count could rise to twice the number and could weigh in excess of a ton. Their abstract artwork also included people, animals and/or scenes from mythology.

Lead Bits & Pieces

An archaeologist once described lead to me as the "silly putty" of the ancient world, and I know exactly what he meant. It is soft, malleable and has a low melting point, all of which means that it has always had a multitude of uses. Some fields seem to be full of small pieces of scrap lead and they too give a great, heart racing, signal.

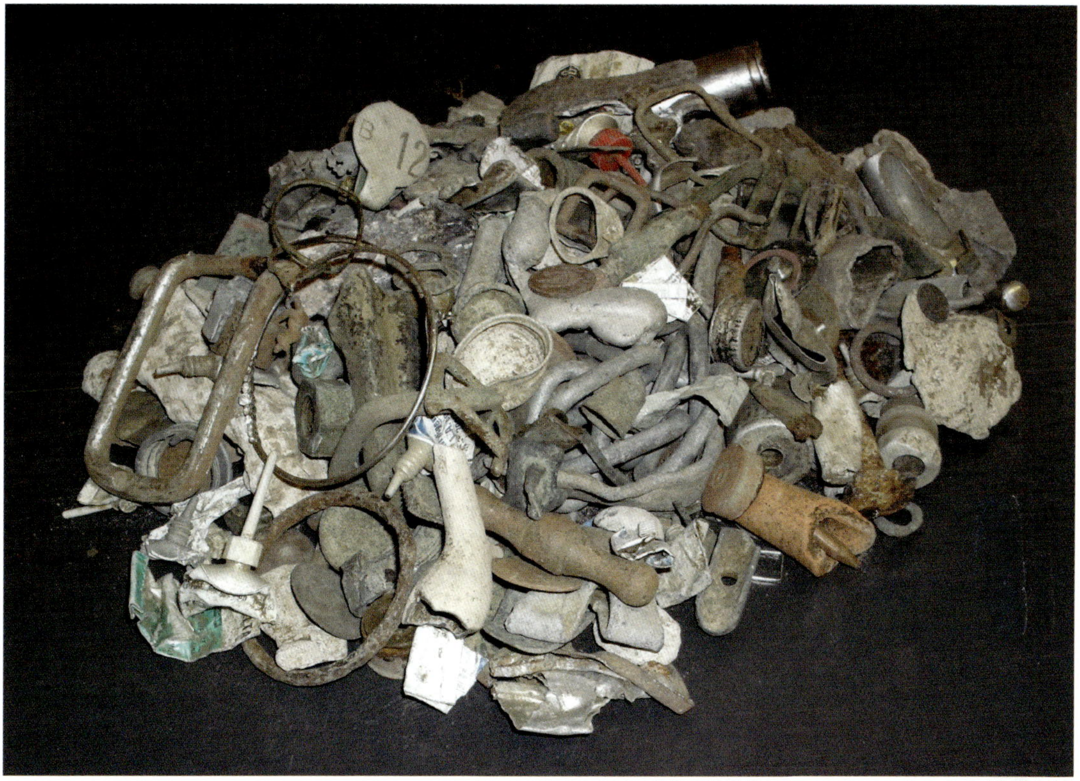

About a year's rubbish finds.

But turn adversity to advantage! For some years our club has been collecting the scrap lead found by members and selling it off to a dealer. It's not a fortune, but we annually raise about £50 for charity and it means that we feel a little better about pulling a chunk of lead from the ground.

Bullets and musket balls.

One level up on the scale of desirable finds (but still pretty low) we come to the objects that come out of the gun. Personally I quite like lead musket balls and, as you can see, they come in different sizes. You often come across one that has impacted and has a flattened edge. Lead bullets of 19th century date, designed for rifles, will impress most farmers (no, really, they will) and then you get the 20th century copper-alloy bullets. I have kept a small collection of these things and, when our club display finds at Young Farmers events, I always put them out. The real farmers go straight past the Roman brooches, pay scant attention to the medieval hammered coins but zoom in on the collection of bullets and shell cases!

The Golden Rule of rubbish is: never assume that it is rubbish until you have got home, examined the object thoroughly, and you are absolutely sure.

This is particularly true when starting out on the hobby, as you will simply not recognise artefacts for what they are. If in doubt, ask your FLO or an experienced detectorist (whose judgement you trust!). Many of us have tales of throwing something away which we later realised should have been kept and recorded!

Finally, remember to pick up items that you can find by just using your eyes as you walk across the fields. This is always better after rain, as the dirt is washed off and the items are normally shiny. The archaeologists call this "fieldwalking" and we do it as a matter of course. This is always better on ploughed land, but items do show up in grass fields from where the moles, badgers and foxes disturb the soil and leave it on top. Neolithic flint arrow heads and scrapers are regularly found on the surface. You might even find bits of tiles from the Dissolution of the Monasteries that occurred in the 1500s. Also to be found is glass from Roman to the present day, and fossils which can date to about 450 million years ago! Who knows what you might find?!

Recording Finds

The whole point of recording your finds is illustrated here with the information already being used from the Frome Hoard, as talked about by Sam Moorhead from the British Museum.

"With 52,503 coins, the Frome Hoard is exceptional by any standards. However, it is also enormously important because Dave (Crisp) enabled us to excavate the hoard professionally, and because it contains the largest group of Carausian coins ever found together. When all the illegible coins have been conserved, we expect to have around 800 coins of Carausius (AD 286-93).

"Carausius came from Menapia, the region around the mouth of the River Rhine. After an early career as a sailor, he rose through the ranks to become a senior general in Germany and Gaul under the emperor Maximian (AD 286-310). Carausius was tasked with commanding the Roman fleet in the North Sea so as to combat the increasing threat from Germanic pirates who were probably

The five silver *denarii* from the Frome Hoard and a selection of bronze radiates, © British Museum. *(Photo Steven Dodd)*

attacking not only Roman settlements on the coast and near major rivers, but also fleets of Roman supply ships which transported grain and other goods from Britain to the Continent. History tells us that Carausius waited for the pirates to attack and then took their booty off them without giving it back to its original owners; for this, Maximian sentenced Carausius to death around the year AD 286.

"Carausius, however, escaped capture and was probably made emperor at Rouen in Northern France where his first coins were struck. So far, one of his Rouen coins has been identified in the hoard. From Rouen, Carausius moved to Britain which became the core of his empire - he probably also held some coastal territory in Gaul. His arrival in Britain is celebrated on two silver denarii in the Frome Hoard: one shows Britannia greeting Carausius with an inscription from the Roman writer Virgil - 'Welcome, O long-awaited one'; the other coin shows Carausius riding into London with the inscription proclaiming his arrival 'ADVENTUS'.

"There are five silver *denarii* of Carausius in the hoard, the largest number ever found in a single find; I only know of just over 300 *denarii* of Carausius in existence. On one of the other coins, Carausius proclaims that he is the 'Renewer of Rome' around an image of the wolf suckling Romulus and Remus. The Frome Hoard, therefore, provides a wonderful insight into Carausius' propaganda campaign.

"All the other pieces in the hoard are bronze 'radiates', some still retaining their silver wash. There are a large number of early coins which do not have mintmarks. These pieces vary enormously in quality, some being of good workmanship, others being very crude. One would expect such variety because Carausius had to set up his mints in Britain from scratch and would not have had access to any official mint staff from the continent. There were two mints in Britain: we know one was at London; the other struck coins marked with a C or G and we just call it 'C' Mint.

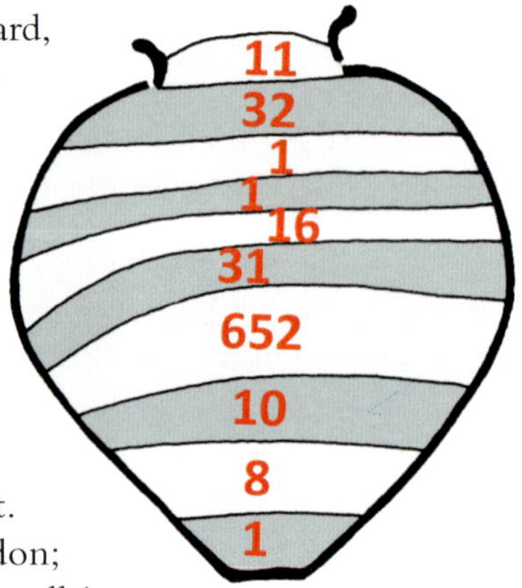

Section drawing of the pot (by Alan Graham) showing the provisional number of Carausian coins in each layer.

"As yet, we do not know where 'C' Mint was, but I will be presenting some new thoughts on this when I publish the new Roman Imperial Coinage volume for Carausius and Allectus. However, because we were able to excavate the Frome Hoard by layers, I know that there were two separate groups of Carausian coins The larger group consists of the later coins; they were tipped into the pot about halfway through the process. However, a smaller group of earlier coins, including the silver *denarii,* were present in the last batch of coins to be added to the hoard; they were found right at the top of the pot. This group has a significant number of early London mint coins marked ML ('Moneta Londiniensis'), but no coins from the 'C Mint'; there are many coins marked with 'C' in the main group of Carausian coins further down the pot. This does appear finally to confirm that London started to mark its coins before 'C Mint'. Amongst the early London coins are some struck to honour the legions which assisted Carausius: one for Legio XX at Chester has its legionary mascot the boar. The majority of the other coins are London coins marked with F O and B E, the latest pieces dating to around AD 290/1 when Carausius repelled an invasion by Maximian - this was the first time ever that a British navy was used to defend our shores. Research into the latest coins is on-going, but it does seem that it will shed light on the possible nature of 'C' Mint

"Amongst the Carausian coins there are a number of new varieties that have not been recorded before. Because it took a while to establish proper quality control in Carausius' mints, there are numerous differences in details and a large number of mistakes - whereas most emperors at the time had around ten to fifteen different versions of the imperial title, Carausius had over a hundred! The Frome Hoard is therefore helping us to define more clearly one of the most complex coinages ever struck in the ancient world; undoubtedly more secrets will be unveiled in the coming years."

Coins of Carausius in the Frome Hoard
Sam Moorhead (Dept. of Portable Antiquities and Treasure, the British Museum) May 24, 2012

"Chance finds made by members of the public have always formed an important part in advancing our knowledge of the past. The advent of the Portable Antiquities Scheme and the Treasure Act has seen a dramatic increase in the number of reported discoveries; hence chance finds form an ever more important part in our understanding of the past. Finds of treasure often receive considerable media coverage but less glamorous finds such as pottery sherds, flints and coins all have a very important contribution to make. Details of many of these finds are uploaded onto the Portable Antiquities website. This is very important, but there is always potential for finds to reveal more as new lines of research are pursued. The donation of finds to museums is to be encouraged, making them available for future research and study. It is very important that significant discoveries are investigated archaeologically, particularly if they are in, or come from, an undisturbed context. There have been a number of instances in Somerset that underline the importance of taking this approach. One of the best examples is the 1998 Shapwick Hoard of 9238 denarii which, upon investigation, proved to have been buried below the floor of a room in a previously unrecorded Roman villa.

The Frome Hoard is another classic example of best practice with finder, landowners, archaeologists, coin specialists, conservators and museum curators all working, closely and openly, together in the interest of gaining as much information as possible. As this is being written, detailed work on the study of the Frome Hoard coins is still at a relatively early stage but the benefits of the controlled excavation and retrieval of the coins is apparent, both from the point of view of understanding the circumstances surrounding the hoard's burial and of the placing of the coins in the pot. Much more will be learned as the work progresses."

Steve Minnitt (Head of the Museum of Somerset)

Portable Antiquities and Treasure

Detectorists keep saying that their hobby is the best of them all. Well, I suppose advocates of windsurfing, stamp collecting, and gardening all say the same about what they do! Yet, in one way, detecting truly does have an extra dimension compared with anything else and that is because as well as collecting what we find we have the option to record it too. The act of recording your finds means that you personally are contributing to saving Britain's heritage and helping the experts understand the lives of our ancestors. All of us involved in this book think that is rather magical!

Perhaps we should start with the bit that is not optional! In 1996 the law which defined "Treasure" in England and Wales, was changed, replacing one that could be traced back to the 12th century! It now refers to objects, over 300 years old, which contain 10% silver or gold or other archaeological objects found alongside such an item. It was later amended to include prehistoric hoards. Single coins were omitted but two or more coins, thought to have been originally together, do count, even if the plough has subsequently pushed them apart! A full up to date definition is given in the appendices.

If you find an item that you suspect might be classified as Treasure then you are under a legal obligation to inform the local coroner, although telling your FLO will do just as well as they can pass on the information. The idea behind the law is a

VALUATION COMMITTEE

sensible one (i.e. to save for the nation the most significant, and precious objects, found by the public). Any suspected Treasure item is sent to the BM (or the National Museum of Wales) for examination. If they consider it Treasure then a Coroner's hearing has to "rubber stamp" their view and then the item appears before the Treasure Valuation Committee (TVC), a group of independent experts who meet in the BM to put a market value on an object.

Once a value has been agreed between the TVC, the finder and the landowner, then museums have the right to buy the object at this price and have some months to find the money. However, museums may disclaim the object because they don't want it (or perhaps can't raise the money) and it is then returned to the finder.

The valuations are usually fair (disputes do happen but there is an appeals process) and the system, on the whole, works well. However, it can be very slow (sometimes as much as a couple of years or so) and this is partly because items that qualify as Treasure but are clearly not of the quality to interest a museum clog up the process. The other problems are the need for local hearings (there has been talk of the BM getting a dedicated Treasure Coroner to speed things up) and the sheer success of the scheme! The graph shows how the number of Treasure cases, each year, has dramatically grown - it is a victim of its own success!

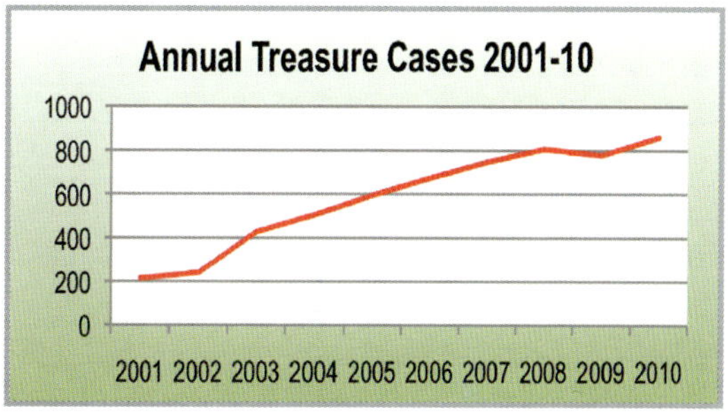

Objects that are not Treasure, yet are still over 300 years old, come under the umbrella of the Portable Antiquities Scheme (PAS). There is no legal obligation to do anything with your finds but the moral case is overwhelming. It all started in 1997 with six pilot schemes where detectorists were encouraged to record objects with archaeologists and, in 2003, the project went national. Today, the scheme funds the work of about 40 Finds Liaison Officers (FLOs) and, behind the scenes, about half a dozen National Finds Advisers. Each of the FLOs is a qualified archaeologist who has had specialist finds training. Their job is to visit metal detecting clubs in their county and record finds as well as deal with independent detectorists and general members of the public who may pop into local museums with unidentified objects.

"Probably the most important aspect of the FLO's job (and the one I certainly enjoy the most!) is identifying and recording the huge variety of

objects discovered by metal detectorists. One minute it may be an 'eyes only' prehistoric flint tool and the next, a Roman coin, medieval buckle or early medieval (Anglo-Saxon) dress accessory. Whatever the object, it is important that we record it in as much detail as we possibly can so this information can be saved on our online database (www.finds.org.uk/database) for all to see and use. This means, in the very least, we take measurements, weight and a photograph; but almost as important as the object itself is knowing where it came from, and we ask finders to provide us with precise and accurate find spots (which the general public will not see more precisely than a four-figure grid reference or 1km square). This creates an ever-growing map of information across England and Wales."
Katie Hinds, Wiltshire Finds Liaison Officer

The photograph shows our Wiltshire FLO, Katie Hinds, dealing with a club member at one of our meetings. She takes into her care all the finds (giving receipts!) and, two months later, returns them with a written report on each. FLOs also attend rallies, give talks, visit schools and, increasingly, arrange for detectorists to help on archaeological digs in the area.

Katie Hinds, Wilts FLO, at a club meeting recording finds.

The one thing they don't do is give valuations. It is not part of their job; they are not interested in the value, and they probably don't have the foggiest anyway.

The Finds Advisers provide expert backup to the FLOs. Each has their own area of expertise and, they too, act as an interface between detectorists and academic archaeologists.

The PAS exists, according to Roger Bland, Head of the PAS at the British Museum, *"to minimise the loss of our heritage caused by the failure to record systematically objects found by the public."*

The crowning glory of the PAS is the database at www.finds.org.uk and this should become one of your favourite websites! The number of objects recorded is pushing one million and is going up by about 100,000 every year and, of these, about 90% have been found by detectorists. The database was revamped in 2010 and this has made it much more user friendly, particularly as most entries now have attached images. Anyone can access this material, although precise find location is deliberately withheld from the general public; and it can be fascinating looking at similar objects to those that you have just found yourself!

So why should you, the new detectorist, bother with all of this? Because, while the ownership of the object itself is shared between you and the landowner, the information it can tell us is part of our heritage - it belongs to all of us. Removing objects from the ground and then keeping quiet about them destroys that heritage; it reduces the story of who we are and where we have come from - a sort of cultural theft.

"A major survey of metal detecting, in 1995, found only eleven Bronze Age references. By 2008 there were 6683 in East Anglia alone!" - Nisha Doshi, University of Cambridge Master's Thesis.

Yet this only works if the academics can make use of all this material and add to the story of these islands. Is the PAS really helping with this? The short answer is "Yes!", and that this is really taking off. On the PAS website there is a summary of the number of academic research projects currently directly using the PAS database. The numbers are increasing every year and, at the time of writing, they are 62 PhD projects and 85 MA projects.

This must represent a high proportion of all the research being done in the UK and can only mean that the effort of recording finds is really making a significant difference to our knowledge of the past! So why is the database proving so popular? For the older generation of archaeologists it has taken a while to get past the suspicions of working closely with detectorists, but that is fading and they are waking up to the wonderful resource that the database provides. There has also been an inevitable time lag, in that the database becomes increasingly useful as it gets bigger and the statistics it provides become more reliable. For example by 2010, and in Lincolnshire alone, 175 new archaeological sites had been discovered because of finds recorded with the PAS. Better still, for the younger generation it is becoming the most natural thing in the world to get help from detectorists and the database is simply invaluable. A PhD student who makes use of our recording now will think favourably of the hobby for the rest of their professional career!

Sam Moorhead, National Finds Adviser for the PAS says, *"Across Britain, the PAS records are identifying large, poorly defined rural [Roman] settlements which have previously lain undetected."* He believes that the recording of Roman coins by detectorists is transforming our understanding of Roman Britain. Archaeological digs have always focussed on high status villas or military forts, yet the PAS gives on rural sites which have been badly under-represented before now. He is insistent that we should even record our "grots" as these can help give a more accurate picture of coin use across the period.

Anyone who uses a metal detector in England and Wales has access to a unique resource - the Portable Antiquities Scheme - to help them record their finds and thus add to our understanding of our past. This has helped to break down the barriers between metal detecting and archaeology that existed before the Scheme started in 1997.

As Roger Bland informs us, in 2006 a Code of Practice on Responsible Metal Detecting in England and Wales which was endorsed by both the national detecting bodies and all the leading archaeological bodies provided a clear set of guidelines for detector users to follow http://finds.org.uk/getinvolved/guides/codeofpractice

The Scheme was founded to record archaeological objects found by members of the public in England and Wales, and has had national coverage since 2003. There is a network of 40 locally-based Finds Liaison Officers, 5 National Finds Advisers and 4 other staff based at the British Museum (details of your local FLO can be found at http://finds.org.uk/contacts). In addition to recording finds, the FLOs play an important role in helping finders report their finds under the Treasure Act and in advising them on the process.

Neither the PAS nor the 1996 Treasure Act applies in Scotland or Northern Ireland however regrettable that might be. In Scotland any objects can be claimed by the Crown under the law of bona vacantia. I do not have any experience of how this works in practice but more information can be found at www.treasuretrovescotland.co.uk/

In Northern Ireland the situation is different again and, unless you have a licence, it is an offence to excavate land searching for archaeological objects.

Treasure Valuation Committee

I have personally been through the Treasure process four times before my finding of a Roman hoard (described later). As I have stated before, I am fully convinced that it is a fair system. Back in the old days I was at a rally down in Essex when I found a very nice medieval (13th-14th century) silver annular brooch. As the inquest was about a hundred miles away, I conducted it by post and it was straight forward Treasure. The valuation came in initially as a bit low so I thought I would challenge it, and the final price came back a little more. Maybe it was my challenge, or maybe they just thought the initial price was a bit low.

Medieval brooch, my first Treasure item.

Then, in 2005, I found a very nice Saxon (or should that be early medieval) silver pyramidal mount, down in Somerset. I have to say I was not sure what it was until one of the members said there was a picture of one in the Treasure Reports. This was a slightly later, Anglo-Saxon version (6th-7th century) as it has a bar across the bottom for a strap which stopped his knife falling out of his sheath. It's believed they were just a fashion accessory - a bit like "bling" is today.

A Saxon pyramid mount, and the bar on the underside.

A few years ago I was also very lucky to find two Roman silver rings in the same week in Wiltshire. One was quite plain but the other had a nice orange carnelian stone in it with a picture of a bird sitting on a branch This ring came to a sad ending. It had a bad kink in it, where the plough must have hit it one year. But the ring was full of dirt, and as I gently removed the dirt under the tap a piece of the ring fell out. Remember the old maxim: if in doubt leave it alone.

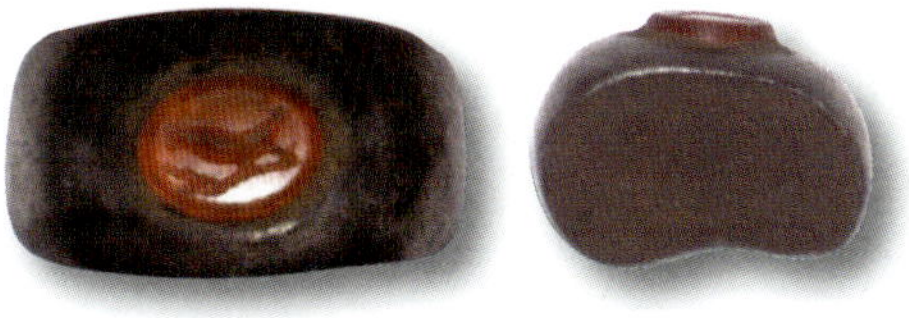

Roman silver ring with intaglio, and the bad crack underneath.

But all was not lost I had saved the bits, but this must have affected the value from the TVC. The British Museum still wanted it for their collection. (Why I don't know). I did mention by letter that all it needed was a bit of soldering, maybe they did get it fixed.

Crosby Roman cavalry helmet.

There are exceptions to the rule, like the Crosby Roman cavalry helmet sold at Christies for £2.3 million but there is always somebody who is willing to pay over the odds for a unique item. This was estimated by Christies at £200,000 to £300,000 .

It's like a nice gold Roman ring with an Indigo of Alexandria the Great just sold in America. Normally a ring like this would be valued at about £2,000 to £3,000. Somebody wanted that one and paid $55,000 - it's a funny world.

These were all long procedures but I have always found once the Inquest is over then it does move along at quite a good pace. (Well for a bureaucracy department anyway). All my four items took about a year, from start to finish.

So overall with these four valuations from the Treasure Valuation Committee I believe they were fair. But you will always have somebody who tells you that you could have got more for it, if the item had gone to auction.

But remember if the item was returned, and was put into private auction, you would still have to pay commission etc. before receiving your money. What payment you get from the Treasure Valuation is yours to do with as you like.

Cleaning, Conserving and Researching Finds

If there is one subject that is guaranteed to get professional archaeologists blowing a gasket it is the approach of metal detectorists towards the cleaning and conservation of objects they find. As a chemist, I have to admit they have a point! So here is a simple guide to what the metal detectorist can safely do and what you should avoid like the plague.

Always start with a close visual inspection of the object. Try to decide what metal it is made of and how fragile it is. Copper alloys like bronze (copper and tin) or brass (copper and zinc) go green in the soil and, in the case of Georgian copper coins, an ugly dark brown colour. Silver can be anywhere between "silver" and black, entirely depending on the soil conditions. Lead is very dense, quite soft and usually goes white in the ground, unless it is a quite recent loss.

If the object is in a precarious state you ought to do nothing at all until it has been recorded. Both of us have broken ancient objects through being over eager, and neither of us is proud of it. Restrain yourself from doing any cleaning, bending, scratching or any form of intervention when in the field - bad things can quickly happen, and it is a shame if an object has survived for a thousand years in the soil only for you to break it within a minute of discovery. Take a deep breath and keep it safe until you get home!

Make yourself a cleaning kit like the one shown in the photograph. It is very simple and is *all* you need to do a good job. The components are: tap water and a bit of washing up liquid (other brands are available!); an old

Basic cleaning kit.

soft tooth-brush; cotton swabs (a must); wooden toothpicks; and some sort of deep tray, plastic being much better than aluminium.

Never wash anything under a running tap as you might break a piece off or even wash something down the sink. Don't laugh, for it really happens! Instead, put some tepid (not hot) water in your tray, with just a touch of detergent, and wash with your fingers. If the object is gilded be very careful indeed. Use the toothbrush gently. If you have a plastic tray then you can leave the object to soak, but not in an aluminium one as you will start off a chemical reaction which you really don't want.

Afterwards you can use the swabs to safely remove extra dirt. Be patient as it can take quite a time to remove all the dirt from a Roman coin. One of the golden rules of conservation is never to let two different metals be in contact with each other so this is why the toothpicks are so useful. If you want to pick out dirt or even small bits of corrosion then a metal needle will badly scratch the object and is not very good anyway. However, you can use the wooden toothpick without doing any damage to the metal, as long as you take your time and are not too aggressive!

Wash your hands after cleaning metal objects. Heavy metals are toxic, and lead is the worst!

Should I straighten my hammered coin? A surprising number of hammered coins are found bent to different degrees and this always tempers the joy of finding one. It is much more satisfying to display a flat coin so, inevitably, the temptation is to think about straightening it. But should you? Well before you do anything, clean it up as best you can and try and identify it. If it's rare and valuable then don't even think about it! There are experts who, for a fee, will safely do this sort of thing for you, and if you snap it yourself then you will feel more than miserable.

Badly bent hammered coin before and after.

If the coin is not particularly unusual, then look at the metal. Gold will bend fairly easily but your coin is much more likely to be silver and this can be very brittle. Can you already see small cracks? If so, leave it alone. If not, and you are determined to "have a go" then photograph the object first (so you have a record before you ruin it) and put the coin in some hot water for a few minutes. Get two flat blocks of wood, or a couple of heavy books, and put some kitchen towel, or soft cloth, on them. Place the coin between them and apply some gentle yet firm pressure. Stop after a few moments, check the coin for cracks, reheat it and do it all again. Eventually it will either straighten or break!

Should I use silver polish on my coin? If it's of any value you will instantly halve that value. If it's not, then it's up to you, but personally I would never do this.

What should I do with Roman grots? After cleaning, decide if the coin is simply worn by being in circulation for a long time, or corroded by chemical reaction in the soil. There is nothing to be done to reverse the wear on a coin but there are a few things you can do about corrosion. Use a toothpick to remove any loose pieces. If it's a valued coin then all you should then do is stabilise the coin against further corrosion, usually by storing it in a dry place. There are coin "dips" on the market, and these are fine to use if you can afford them.

However, that should be the limit of your home chemistry! There are many, many amateur conservators out there each with their own foolproof way of cleaning up an old coin. Most of these techniques are ineffective, some damaging to the object, and a few downright dangerous! Don't go using vinegar or lemon juice in an attempt to clean the coin, and don't wrap coins in aluminium foil. Also, in my own view, do not go anywhere near ultrasound cleaners which, in my experience, cause far more damage than they reverse. Worst of all, do not try anything like electrolysis (i.e. using a battery and trying to reverse the corrosion). Try that with a salt solution and you will poison yourself with chlorine gas!

My one concession is the use of a barrelling machine, which will cost about £70. But only barrel your grottiest coins that otherwise can give no information at all, and are of no value. These can clean up quite well and might enable you to identify an emperor or two. Such coins then make great gifts for children - perhaps as educational Christmas stocking fillers for younger members of the family?

Is there nothing else I can do to improve the appearance of my objects? On a badly worn coin, particularly one which is quite dark in colour, the application of a little Vaseline can highlight the features; but ensure that the coin is completely dry before doing this as otherwise you can trap small amounts of moisture that will corrode the metal. One tip that was given to me, and which works well for regimental badges, is to apply the smallest amount of brown shoe polish and rub it in as

Barrelling machine.

CLEANING – LEAST IS BEST

this, too, highlights detail. The point is that both of these methods are reversible and should not cause damage to a dry object.

General Coin Conservation

"At the British Museum our purpose for the Treasure process is to make coins identifiable without losing contextual information. Coins are examined for remains in the corrosion which might be the only evidence of a cloth bag or leather purse, etc. We aim to process hoards within a year of their arrival but the increased numbers being found has resulted in a huge backlog. Hoards, like Frome, jump the queue if they arrive wet as they are the most vulnerable to deterioration. Unfortunately, now even damp hoards have to wait their turn, stored in refrigerated conditions to inhibit mould growth while maintaining their humidity as wet deposits are easier to clean off than those that have dried on. Coins discovered in a pot are removed layer by layer as we have learnt that many hoards were put together sequentially or from different sources, the ratio of coin types being different from top to bottom."

Pippa Pierce, Conservator at the British Museum

Finally, may I recommend a couple of publications? Firstly, on the left, a very useful (free!) little booklet produced by the PAS and aimed at metal detectorists; your friendly FLO should be able to get you a copy. If you want to know more about the subject, then there is this more detailed conservation guide (see appendix "Further Reading" for full details).

Two books to read before doing anything else than washing a find.

Displaying Finds

I think displaying finds is very important, but it is an area where some detectorists lose the plot! To look at a well-constructed display of your best finds can give you pleasure years after you found them, and makes it easier to bore friends and family with your tales of epic discovery. However, after all the effort of buying the kit, getting permissions and spending endless hours finding nothing but cow pats, many detectorists just put their prizes in a plastic bag and forget them! What a shame!

One easy solution for coins is the use of special stacking trays that can be bought from companies like Lindner. To give a little information on each item, I always include a little square of card with, on the front, a brief statement of what the object is and, on the back, when and where I found it along with the PAS database reference. You can also get cases, which are quite similar. These trays can also be used for small artefacts - anything from rings to coin weights - but they do have their limits and that is where things get a bit trickier.

Examples of labels and stackable storage cases for coins.

For more bulky, or "three dimensional" items, you might go for a miniature chest of drawers from an antique or second hand furniture shop. Alternatively you can get ready made hinged display cases with glass tops. These can be just the thing if you want to show your items to the public when representing your club; but they might be less than ideal at home! You can use pins to hold items in position - partly to avoid damage and partly to show them off to best effect. However, never use metal pins as this can accelerate corrosion. Instead, use special plastic-coated ones that you will often see in museums - talk nicely to your FLO!

There is no perfect display solution for larger objects, and you could do worse than ask other detectorists what they choose to do!

Researching Finds

I think this is one of the joys of the hobby! As you have no idea what you will find next you will have no idea where your research will take you. Objects tell a story, and it is not just the experts who can get a buzz by finding out what that story is; and in this information age it has never been easier to do!

Books are still the best place to start. After a while you may well accumulate your own collection, or you may well find that your club owns copies of some of the more expensive books (if not, suggest it!). In the appendices we have included a "Further Reading" section that should help you along. When I bought my first machine I was persuaded to buy a copy of Spink's *Coins of England* catalogue and also *Benet's Artefacts*. The two together set me back some £50 but it was money very well spent - I fully recommend that you do the same!

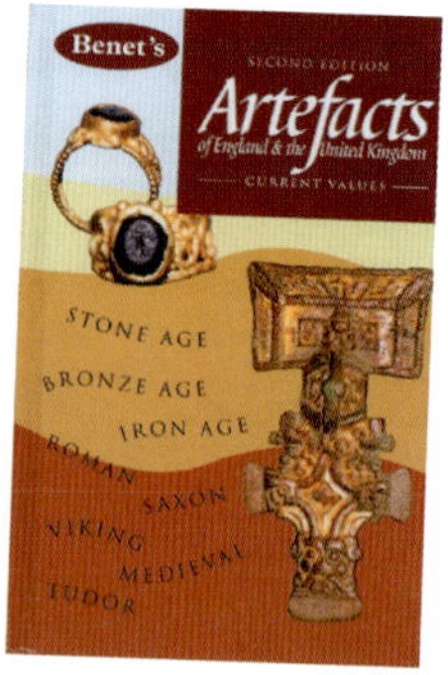

There is a really excellent monthly magazine (*Treasure Hunting*) published about our hobby. For more details go to: www.treasurehunting.co.uk

A year's subscription would be an ideal way to learn about the hobby and would make a good birthday or Christmas present if wife/husband or other relative is fishing for ideas! You will read thoughtful and informative articles, learn about up-coming rallies and, most importantly, see lots of finds and learn to recognise them.

There are also several "popular archaeology" magazines available, which might be of interest to some people. They will often

MAGAZINES – ALWAYS A GOOD READ

include items of interest to metal detectorists, particularly if you want to learn more about the context of your finds. The best-selling of these is *Current Archaeology* (www.archaeology.co.uk)

When recording your finds that are over 300 years old with the PAS (and yes, we do want you to do that!), your FLO will write a little report for you about the object. The length (and quality) of these can vary, but at their best can give you a superb understanding of the object and its context - and you haven't had to do any of the work! These reports will usually cite academic references that the FLO has used for research, and if you are really keen, or just a bit of a nerd like me, you could always get these references yourself!

Of course, we then must come to the Internet and so I must start by stating the obvious - that any idiot can write anything about an object and it may be utter tosh. So be careful what you read (and believe)! Club sites often have photos of finds posted along with information and this can be useful. There are also commercial sites, both here and in the States, which can give images and descriptions.

However, the one site you must become familiar with is the PAS database on www.finds.org.uk

In its early form this was quite hard to use, but it has got a lot better, and the sheer number of objects posted (nearing a million) allows you to look at images, and approximate find spots, of objects just like yours. To give you a real example of this, in Chapter 9 there is an image of a late Saxon "mask" pendant. When I found this I had never seen a parallel, but after half an hour on the PAS site I had found 11 similar objects and plotted their find spots (almost all in Wiltshire and Hampshire, which was interesting). There are also 13,000 images of Roman brooches although I wouldn't fancy checking them all!

The PAS site also has little "essays" written for detectorists by BM staff on subjects including Roman coinage and medieval hammered, and these are well worth reading (and printing off). There are also several metal detecting chat rooms where photos of objects can be exchanged and views asked for. This is a great thing, but be wary of "certain" identifications and remember that this is not a substitute for recording with the PAS!

There is another type of research you can do, and that is to research the land where you are detecting. You might choose to do this before you get permission to detect, after permission but before detecting, or after the finds start appearing (perhaps to investigate a particular field). Nowadays your first stop ought to be Google Images to check for any crop marks that appear in aerial photographs. What is a crop mark, I hear you ask? Well, ground that has been disturbed by the building of a wall, for example, will always have a different make up from the ground on either side, even long after the wall has disappeared. This might make it retain water better, or worse, and mean that crops grow at a faster, or slower, rate along the line of the long lost wall. So, in times of drought, a photograph taken from the air will see a line of greener crop (or yellower crop) compared to the background. Hence, deserted buildings can give themselves away and this might be a good place to search!

Then there are maps - new and old! A modern OS map (always use the "orange" 1:25,000 as they show field boundaries) will show footpaths and these can easily be medieval, and might have been busy thoroughfares between villages. Your farmer ought to be able to provide you with a copy of the farm map and, with a bit of luck, this might have individual field names on it. These could give you a clue about an earlier use for the land.

Finally, you can always visit your county records office where detailed maps will be found back to the 18th century or even earlier. If you've never done this sort of thing before don't worry, as you will find the staff will fall over themselves to be helpful and to show you the ropes! It might be an idea to ring them in advance to see if they have the material you want, or any ideas of their own!

Upgrading to a More Expensive Machine

A top of the range Lamborghini - in hobby terms like a £2,000 detector.

The world is your oyster, so why not, before you start out as a detectorist, just buy the most up-to-date and the most expensive machine? For the same reason as when you pass you're driving test, you don't rush and buy a Lamborghini car! A Lamborghini could cost $1,600,000, take 3.3 seconds to reach 60 mph and it has a top speed of 211 mph. Nice car, but could you drive it, enjoy it, and get the best out of it?

I don't think so, and that's what we are trying to show in this book; start slow, get the best from your chosen machine, enjoy the hobby, and then, when you are hooked, maybe change your machine for a more expensive one. You might also be surprised that you don't want to change and, even if you do, you keep your old one just as a backup. By the time you are ready to change, you will be familiar with a lot of the machines that are available from the manufactures, and the dealers. (P.S. I wouldn't mind trying out the car though!)

So which machine is next? Let's look at the choice. All you have to do is pick up a copy of *Treasure Hunting* and you will find about a dozen manufacturers, each with six to ten machines on offer!

That's about 90 detectors and, even if you eliminate the starter machines and those at the very top end, that might still leave 45 odd machines to tempt you. This next detector is going to cost you about £500 so you will want to get it right, first time. I have known lads, over the years, change their machines two or three times in quick succession, far too readily, and each time losing money on the deal.

So how do you go about picking one from all that are available?

The very best way is to talk to other detectorists, but even this way you still have to cut through the bull.

Upgrading to a More Expensive Machine

ALWAYS TAKE ADVICE

Detectorists are like fishermen, as it just gets better every time they tell it! You always talk up the machine you are using, and then knock it against the new one you have just bought!

I still have my last two machines; they still work well and, every now and again, I take them out and use them, just for old times sake. I digress; talk to other members of your club, or people at a rally as it's better to have too many opinions than none at all. Talk to a few dealers, who are there to sell you a machine and give you advice. Most will go that extra mile to ensure you get the correct detector for you.

Try out a couple of machines, and this is one of the many advantages of being a member of a club. If there is a machine you really fancy, ask somebody if you can borrow it for a day or two. If they are a bit reluctant, then go out detecting together. They won't mind giving you a demonstration and a few pointers and they would probably let you try it out then for an hour or two. If they don't, buy one anyway and tell them it was £100 cheaper than theirs!

We are not going to tell you which machine to upgrade to, as there are too many excellent manufactures, but I have to fill this page with something so let me run through my own history of buying detectors! It started over 25 years ago with an original 770 from C.Scope. Later I went on to a lighter machine, the Fisher 1265; next came the classic Laser BI; I then tried a Tesoro Rapier, a nice light machine which I bought because I had a bad arm at the time but, within a year, and as soon as my arm got better, I went back to the B1 and used that for years; it's still a classic machine in my eyes.

I bought a Minelab Explorer II when it came home to me that others were getting signals on targets which I was missing. So I have bought six machines in this time frame, and this gives an average of about 4 years each, and I think that's about right.

So when it's time to upgrade look at the main manufacturers, consider your budget; ask others what they have and if their find rate, on all types of farms, is good. Ask them about the amount of rubbish they dig; talk about discrimination and if the pinpointing works well.

(A few years ago, on a display day, one of the lads gave us a demonstration of a great new machine he had just bought. He ended up with a hole about one and a half feet across and a foot deep. He did find a pound coin in the end, but that "good" machine was clearly rubbish at pinpointing!)

Talk to the members who always seem to have finds on the monthly display table and ask how often they go out. If they go out detecting a lot more than others then they should have more finds, but if not see what machine they use! In a club there should be a fair spread of different machines but if one machine, or manufacturer, is more popular - ask why!

So, what should your next machine be capable of? Shown here are the contents of a small pit, 10 inches down and with a lot broken and burnt Roman pottery. There were also a few bits of lead; two bronze late Roman coins (with a 5p added for scale); about 20 rusty iron nails, and a small bit of a Roman silver spoon. This is a lot to ask of any detector as it has to distinguish the good items from the rusty nails.

The contents of a Roman rubbish pit.

We would always recommend you buy a known brand of machine from a good dealer or straight from the manufacturer. *Treasure Hunting* magazine also takes adverts from people trading up. But remember there are plenty of stolen detectors out there, and there are many "grey" imports where you will have no comeback if it fails. I saw a large advert, for an odd machine, in a paper a few months ago that stated it was used by "all major treasure hunters"! It looked like a 1960s toy, and the model has never been listed by our dealers. Or why not buy a pair of detecting sandals, which were advertised in a national paper! It's true - I had a reporter ring me up and ask if I had ever had a pair! There is also a hand held, long range (their words) detector that will, apparently, find treasure (their word) two miles away (Wow! - my word). Don't be fooled by this sort of thing! If you just want to get rid of £500, give it to a charity and stay with the detector you have!

Remember it takes time, as much as six months of frequent use, to get used to a new machine as they are all slightly different. When you have a new machine persevere with it, lay out your finds and listen to the sounds; check the readings. Don't give up and go back to your old detector; accept that you are going to have to learn all over again, but the time spent doing this will be well worth it!.

Some of these manufacturers were in at the very beginning of the hobby and others arrived much later, but they all make machines that are trusted. We cannot recommend a model but if you stay with the companies listed in the appendix then you will not go too far wrong. Happy hunting!

Not One Hoard, But Two!

Romans burying the hoard.
(Picture reproduced courtesy of Victor Ambrus, illustrator on Channel 4's Time Team)

This is my story of the Frome Hoard; why I was there; how the excavation happened over three days; the many people involved in the last eighteen months; the coins themselves; the emperors; and how it has all changed my life.

Metal detecting is my hobby but since the find I have met quite a few archaeologists and academics and, on the whole, I have got on well with them. So why did I find this hoard? Why did it then capture the imagination of people across the world? Why did the publicity carry on for as long as it has? I am going to try to explain what I know happened in 2010 and what I think happened in the Roman period at the time of the pot's burial. I hope you enjoy reading about my discovery of the largest single hoard of Roman coins ever!

I have been detecting seriously since 1982 when I needed a hobby to help me relax: my wife reminded me that I had tried metal detecting once before, and suggested I try it again. I bought myself a basic metal detector and started, slowly, to learn about using it. I only changed my machine when I had mastered that one, and then only for a better one.

One of the first things I did was to join one of the organisations; but that one did not sit well with me and I left. Instead I joined a small local club which, the next year, became part of the Western Federation of the National Council Metal Detecting. I am still in the Trowbridge club, and we are still in the Western Region of the NCMD. Our club members are a good mix of young and old and a better set of like-minded people you could not wish to meet. I am very lucky to have 10 farms where I have the trust of the landowners to detect whenever I like, and our Trowbridge club land on top of that. What more could a metal detectorist want?

Just Another Day Detecting

It was a sunny warm day in April 2010 that changed my life. I had a day off, from my job as a hospital chef, down here in the West Country, and I decided to go out for a day's detecting. Arriving at one of my farms down in Somerset bright and early (well, about 10am - when you have all day there's no point in rushing about!) I parked up on top of the hill and I could see that one of the far fields that the farmer had ploughed was ready for seeding. That's the one for today, I thought. Ploughed and rolled is as good as it gets, so after kitting up, and checking the batteries on my Minclab detector, I started to cut across the two grass fields detecting as I went. One of these fields had yielded a *siliqua* in 2009 and an odd broken Hadrian a

A sunny day in a field in Somerset, April 2010.

bit before that; but nothing else - not a bronze coin of any sort, or any artefact at all. Coming into the second field I got a sharp clear signal and, on my Explorer II, that normally means a good find.

The First Siliqua

After digging down 2 inches there, in my hand, was a silver Roman *siliqua*! This was a beautiful late 4th century coin (Valens AD 364-78). It had a small crack in it and a little clipping, but was still a fantastic find.

The first coin of the first hoard (Valens).

I was out by myself that day, as Tony was working, so I tried to send him a photo on my phone just to wind him up. Unfortunately, it wouldn't send! As stated earlier I had found a *siliqua* the year before, but this was recovered a lot further up the field. I now had a second, but without giving it much thought I went on detecting. I had only walked about 2 feet, and then bang, I had another. That really stopped me in my tracks! I now had three silver Roman coins all of the same type, *siliquae*, and all approximately the same date. This could only mean one of two things: a purse loss, or a scattered hoard.

This really started my heart pumping, and in the next few hours I found about 20 similar Roman coins, each giving me a good signal even though some of them were 7-8 inches down. Mixed in with them were a few broken bits, some only quarters, but giving very quiet although clear signals. By the end of that day I found about 30 coins in total including the bits. This was the best day's detecting I had ever had! For somebody who is into Roman, this was the pinnacle of my detecting years. You can't get much better than a scattered hoard of Roman silver coins! Or so I thought.

Later on that day, before I went home, I stopped and showed my finds to the farmer, Geoff, who was doing the milking at the time. I reminded him that I had to report them to the Coroner, as they would certainly come under the new Treasure law. He was very pleased and interested as they were nice looking silver Roman coins, and he has always been attracted to the history of the farm. But he wasn't as pleased as I was and, of course, he had to get back to the cows and the milking.

Later that evening I got in touch with Katie Hinds, Wiltshire's FLO who records all my finds. I just told her I had found a few Roman silver coins, and I would bring them in for recording at the next meeting, and I had already informed the Somerset Coroner by letter. That evening as soon as I had done all this I sent Tony an

Some of the first hoard of silver *siliquae*.

e-mail of one of the coins just to wind him up a bit. He e-mailed, back "nice coin", and a few extra choice words. I replied back "Sorry, I forgot to say I found 30." The phone rang within less than a minute! I think he was pleased for me, but I didn't know some of the big words he used!

Later the next week I went back again, and found another 20 odd coins. But by now the only signals were very faint, from just a few deep broken coins, and although the Explorer was still giving a good response, I was getting further away from the area of the main hoard.

In the middle of this area, however, I did find a rather nice little bronze piece of twisted wire; at one this had been thickly gold plated and looks like a child's bracelet. This might turn out to be medieval, but you know experts: you get two who say yes, and two more will say no, and another will sit on the fence. Eventually this was returned to me by the present Somerset FLO unrecorded, as it was deemed to be "just a bit of wire".

Personally, given it is two twists of bronze wire, carefully silver soldered together to form a bracelet and then gold plated, I don't think this came off a barbed wire fence!

Bronze bracelet - or is it just a bit of wire?

The Day That Changed My Life

On the third day I returned, still searching the rough area where most of the coins had come from, but by now I had moved about 100 metres away from the main find spot. It was midmorning and I was finding very little, just a couple of broken bits when I had a funny signal. It was very faint, and not very clear; my display was jumping around and not locking on at all.

Now the Explorer II is a really great machine but, like all detectors, it can be fooled by deep iron, and that's just what I thought it was. But after 22 years of detecting I just had to check it out. I carefully cut my normal hole, about 7 inches square, and flapped it back on its uncut side. There was nothing in the divot, and no increase in sound. Six inches down in this small hole there was still nothing, and after another spadeful of soil and a further six inches, still nothing. It was time to get out my small probe, which is ideal for when you cannot find the target; but there was no signal from it either. By this time I was convinced that it was a bit of deep iron, and I was cursing iron, large horseshoes, ploughshares, and blacksmiths in general.

I took yet another spadeful and there was still nothing in the spoil heap except a few bits of clay, showing I was well into the subsoil. I therefore got down on my knees and tried the probe again. At last there was a slight signal, showing that my find only 2 inches away at the most. It was time for the gentle approach, and out came my knife. I gently prized up a large chunk of the thick yellow clay and found just a small piece of black pottery stuck to it - but no metal. I could see that this was a piece of Roman black burnished ware pottery, but this is nothing unusual as there are always bits in any field that's near a Roman road.

I tried again and gently pulled out another handful of the sticky clay. As I turned it over, there, stuck to it, was one very small Roman "grot" coin. Green and grotty yes, but it was still a Roman coin, a small radiate. I was down a long way for a single small Roman coin to give a signal, so I pulled out another handful of clay; stuck on this piece were about 10 more of these small bronze radiate coins, and a few more bits of pottery!

The first few Roman radiates, and bits of pot from the top of the container.

It was at this point that I realised I had found another Roman hoard, and I just sat back on my heels and shouted, "I've done it again!" In over 28 years of detecting I had just found two hoards in three detecting days! I quickly realised that this was obviously a pot of coins that hadn't seen the light of day for at least 1700 years, and was so deep that it hadn't been touched by a plough. It must be completely intact, except for the broken black top, as the clay above it had not been disturbed!

A Day To Remember

"Well that's a turn up for the book!" I thought, "But what do I do now?" My first instinct was to dig further, but common sense prevailed. I knew the academics (archaeologists, historians and coin experts) would wet themselves just thinking about a coin hoard in situ ("still in the ground" to you and me!). Also, as a club we always strongly encourage our members to record finds with the PAS (Portable Antiquities Scheme), so how could I, as Secretary, not do the same?

It was a struggle as I had visions of dozens of metal detectorists stumbling over my hole while I was away. They always say that gold sends people funny, and I think my pot of bronze coins did this for me for a few minutes that day. Then I calmed down and started to think clearly. I was in the middle of nowhere; the pot has been there for about 1,800 years; only the farmer was going to know about it, and nobody else would know exactly where it was. What was the chance of somebody else finding it again in the next few days? However, it was one of the hardest decisions I have ever made. I did not know exactly what I had found; it could have been the size of a small beer pot with a few hundred coins or something larger.

Not One Hoard, But Two!

Reporting Treasure

Before I went home, I went again to see my farmer friend Geoff to let him know what I had found. I had to pull him out of his cowshed again (he must live in there) and I showed him the few bits of black burnished ware, and the Roman grots, which were still mixed in with the clay. He wasn't very impressed as, let's face it, they didn't stack up to the silver *siliquae* that he had seen a few days before. "But there's a pot of them!" I explained, and he seemed more impressed at that, as he was always interested in the local history, and what sort of people lived on the land before him. So before he went back to his cows, he agreed to calling in the archaeologists and to let them dig up whatever was there.

What I showed Geoff before washing the dirt off.

The FLOs

Here in Wiltshire, in our club, we work closely with our Finds Liaison Officer, Katie Hinds. Katie comes along to ever other one of our meetings to record our finds. So I gave her a ring to let her know that I had found a few more of the *siliquae* and, when she had calmed down, I just dropped it into the conversation that I had also found a pot with Roman coins, and they appeared to be radiates. I also told her that I had left it in the ground, and would somebody like to come along and dig it up?

She was very excited about my news, and said she would have to inform the Somerset FLO, Anna Booth, about what I had found, due to it being in Somerset. At the same time I again informed the local coroner of the new events, as the Treasure Act requires.

Alan taking his first shovelful, while I stand by looking bored.

Alan the archaeologist in his hole with Aaron, Katie and Anna watching on.

I had seen a few archaeologists on the telly and had seen how they always seem to push detectorists into the background, if they allowed them to get a look in at all, and only very occasionally credit us with finds. I was determined not to be sidelined, so I gave Katie the dates that I would be available, as I realised they could do nothing without me! When she got back to me she had arranged for the pot to be excavated on my day off from work, just over a week later. We never dreamt at this point that it was going to take three days of digging. They arranged for an archaeologist to meet us at the site on the Thursday at 8 o'clock. I was a little apprehensive about this as I had never really met one, just seen some on television.

I should not have been so cautious as, on the day, Bob Croft of Somerset Council had hired a private archaeologist (Alan Graham) to do the work, and he turned out to be a really pleasant bloke who knew his job well, and didn't at all come across with a high-handed attitude. He was assisted on that day by the two FLOs - Katie Hinds and Anna Booth from Somerset. I had never met Anna before but she turned out to be a very pleasant lady.

That First Day

The Thursday turned out to be another clear and sunny day, which was really lucky, for I cannot imagine what would have happened if it had been raining. So initially it was Katie, Anna, Aaron (my grandson), Alan Graham and I involved. I showed them the radiates and the pieces of pottery that I had recovered, and they agreed with my assessment that it was black burnished ware. It was also pointed out that they looked like bits of the base of a small dish and this turned out to be quite relevant!

After the introductions we walked across the field to the area of the find, and I filled them in as to what had happened with the *siliquae* on the last few days, and how I had found those coins. It was very hard to see where I had dug, so I let them walk over it and then called them back. This was a great relief to me, as obviously the hordes of people digging up my pot never materialised! I had let them walk right over the spot just to show how well it was concealed.

Alan in his nice square clean hole - my small original hole showing in the middle.

Pulling up the sod of grass I revealed the spot. Alan quickly formulated a plan to clear a standardised hole (a 1.5 metre square of grass and soil which was about 20cm deep). This entailed cutting and lifting the grass sods, and stacking them for later. Next, he started to clear the soil to reveal the yellow clay; all this took a bit of time as Alan was working carefully. As soon as he could see the clay he started to brush and scrape until all the dirt was gone; then the clay was completely clear of soil with just a few rocks sticking through.

This showed clearly where my small hole went through the clay. The first thing he uncovered was the large horseshoe (my anti-detecting device!). You can also see, in the photo, a circle of yellow clay showing the disturbed ground where the Romans dug the original hole.

Note the correct recovery procedure, only half at a time

Next, Alan put a line across to section my small refilled hole - cutting it in half from corner to corner - and proceeded to carefully clear away the soil on one side. This was a very slow process, as the clay was thick and hard, and Alan was doing the job very carefully. This slowly revealed half of a rim of an upside down broken

The upside-down "dog dish" just showing.

black dish; this is where my bits of black burnished ware came from. This showed the dish, which some people call "dog dishes", as that is what they look like. It was evident that the dish was a form of lid as there was something else underneath. This turned out to be a rim of a container and this is where I had got my few radiates from. Through the bits of broken pottery we could see a few coins, but they were all covered in thick muck from the soil and clay so, in 1700 years, not one had been lost into the soil!

Watching him slowly uncovering the top of the pot as it just got bigger and bigger, the excitement was infectious as we realised how big the vessel was getting. We still could only see the neck, but it seemed to be getting the two FLOs very excited. Then as Alan carefully worked the clay from around the neck, the pot itself started to appear; this also was a lovely very dark blue, nearly black, piece of pottery that was obviously a completely different type of ware from the "dog dish".

Where Alan had started to clean away the clay there appeared a glistening jet black pot that just started to get bigger and bigger. Once he had taken the clay down a bit more, the talking started about how big it was going to get. During all of this time we were taking photos from every angle; there must have been hundreds taken in that Somerset field before we had finished.

By now we had gained a considerable number of onlookers, mostly the family of the farm owners, and everybody was interested to see what the pot was like. The excitement steadily grew! Soon phone calls were being made to the British Museum (BM), in London, and to Somerset County Archaeologist Bob Croft to let him know that the pot was getting bigger by the minute and could be as big as the Cunetio pot.

The Cunetio Hoard was dug up in an old Roman town (Cunetio) just outside of Marlborough, Wiltshire, in the late 1970s. This hoard contained nearly 55,000 coins but that one was in two containers. The finders just dug them up and took them home, and

The Cunetio pot in Devizes.

then proceeded to mix all the coins together losing lots of information. The main pot survived, but the second lead container was thrown away before the archaeologists could record it.

One call by Katie had museum staff in the Wiltshire Heritage Museum in Devizes measuring the Cunetio pot, which was on display after it had been put back together. This was just to check how the pots compared in size, and from what could be seen they were very similar. After a call from Anna, Bob Croft (Somerset County Archaeologist) arrived on site to find out for himself what all the fuss was about.

Alan was still slowly working his way down the top of the pot rim to reveal the walls as they slowly curved outwards and, as he cleared away the clay, a beautiful glossy black wall appeared. It was cracked, into very large pieces, but it still held together just as it was put there all that time ago. This was still the first day and he was, even now, only just working on the other side of the top half of the vessel. From the very beginning photos were taken from all sides to record every aspect of the excavation and Alan was also drawing a detailed diagram as he went down. After Roger Bland, Head of the Portable Antiques Scheme, and Sam Moorhead (Roman Finds advisor) had phoned and asked about the chances of removing the pot whole, it was decided that this was not possible and the coins would have to be removed systematically.

It was now late afternoon and it was obvious that the excavation would continue into a second day, Friday.

Night Guards

It had been fairly obvious later in the day that we would not be finished by nightfall so, after a few phone calls, I arranged cover for my job on the Friday and also for camping equipment to be brought out so that Aaron and I could sleep next to the hole overnight. The pot was covered up with sacking and bubble wrap and everybody else left for the night. The farmer's family stayed on for a while and then left us to it

At this point, when it was starting to get dark, it left just Aaron and I with a fantastic pot that had been there since Roman times. Camping in a field in Somerset, with the shadows from the moon

Our overnight tent, and Aaron on guard duty.

creating a spooky atmosphere, and with the noises of the night all around us, the reality of it all started to sink in. But even then I had no notion of what was to come!

We started to get things organised for the night. There was no way we could stay awake as we were both knackered; it had been a really long day, and there would be another one tomorrow. So after a snack and a hot drink, we just turned in, hoping that I would wake if anybody came into the field. I think those Roman gods were still looking after their pot, as we both got a good night's sleep.

Friday

The next day I was awake at 6am just as it was getting light. Therefore after putting the kettle on and getting dressed, I started to do a little detecting! Aaron, like all youngsters, could sleep for England, and only just got up before the team arrived at 8 o'clock for another day's dig. As soon as they were okay (they didn't really need us) Aaron and I went off to the local café and had a good breakfast. All that fresh air gives you a good appetite!

Alan started by removing the small black dish that was acting as a lid. With it came a few of the loose coins that the dish had been covering. This left

Friday morning, the clean shiny pot with just a few coins removed.

the rim of the pot completely exposed; you could see that the large pot was full to the brim with more coins! This left a nice clear, clean area to work on, and using the same string mark as a guide, Alan started to systematically remove the coins.

The idea was that he would remove a layer at a time, each containing about 600 coins with all the muck attached to them, and put them into a numbered bag. Alan slowly worked his way down the first half still using the string, which was placed across the top as a guide.

Better Than Mushrooms

This was a slow but meticulous way of doing it, and it seemed to take forever! Alan removed the coins into a mushroom box that had been lined with plastic and one of us scooped them up and placed each box full into the numbered bags. Our hands turned green from the colour that was in the mud that surrounded the coins. This was not a good time for eating your sandwiches! By that evening only the bottom half of the pot was left to remove.

One layer of about 600 coins at a time, removed across half of the pot, then bagged up and marked.

Alan was very particular and, at one stage, could not find a missing piece of pottery. Now this piece was about 2 inches long and about 1 inch wide; not a very big piece, but still important. We could see where this small piece should have been, but we could not figure out where it had disappeared to. Alan then had us carefully sifting the soil and running our fingers through the piles of clay fill that had been cut away from around the pot. We still could not find it. Alan was really concerned to think that we had lost it and, after we all had looked for at least an hour, one bright person pointed out that there was a small space just inside the pot, and it could have slipped down inside! And that is where it was. Alan was so pleased to think that it hadn't gone missing!

Seeing the coins coming out over a three day period was fantastic. They were all covered in thick green gunk, and you had a hard job to tell what type of coins they were, but it was fairly obvious that the majority of them were going to be bronze radiates.

Radiates are Roman coins, with the name coming from the "spiked" headdress, or "crown", that the emperor is wearing. These actually represent the rays are from the sun god, Sol, and imply a link between the emperor and the god.

The example shown is of Victorinus, who ruled AD 269-71.

Radiate of Victorinus.

Alan did such a professional job by taking the coins out in a methodical way that later, in the British Museum, they could tell just where in the pot any particular coins came from. This was essential for the recording, and in the later understanding of the hoard.

Friday after just about a quarter of the coins removed.

At each stage of the process photos were taken so a complete set of written and photographic records were available for studying at a later stage. Apart from my 150 odd photos, there were the FLOs taking their own images, other archaeologists, and visitors to the site; and, as if that were not enough, they even employed a professional photographer to come along and make an official record! This must have been the most photographed pot of coins ever found!

By the end of day two, only about three quarters of the coins had been removed. Another night's camping was called for and, as I could not get out of work on the Saturday, Alan kindly offered to sleep on site that Friday night.

By the time I arrived on the Saturday, nearly all the coins had been removed and I saw the last few being taken out; this just then left the bottom half of the pot in the ground. Alan then started to remove this last link with the Roman people who had lived and worked in this place we now call Somerset. Slowly and cautiously he removed each piece, which was then laid on some bubble wrap in another mushroom tray, and carefully packed them away. As much care was taken with this pottery as with the coins themselves.

This produced, at the end of it all, 67 bags of coins, which weighed in at 160 kg which is about the weight of two adults!

A Roman Hole

It was a funny sort of moment as there were so many people there: archaeologists, FLOs, museum services, the landowners, and two of my family; the visitors' kids had been brought along as well! There was a bit of a carnival atmosphere, but at the same time it was all a bit sad. The coins had been removed and bagged, and now the hole where they, and their beautiful black pot, had rested for 1,700 years, was just a hole in the ground.

The Romans had dug this hole about 4 feet long with one end nearly squared off and the rest in an oval shape. Alan followed the line of the original hole as he cleared away the clay to show what they had dug. The empty pot could have then been placed into the hole, and carefully packed with straw and grass around the sides to protect it. Then it was slowly backed-filled with the thick sticky yellow clay, to stop it falling over, until just the rim was left visible. They could then have started to fill this plain storage pot with coins. It must have taken many people to come forward and drop in their coins, maybe tipping them from satchels and panniers. Maybe some just had a few in a purse; maybe some had a sack-full, but they slowly filled the pot. The coins must have come right to the top, until there was no room for any more. They must have done this filling very carefully as we did not find any loose coins in the clay or dirt around the hole.

The shape of the Roman hole dug 1700 years ago.

An offering maybe?

How many people did it take to give their savings? We just don't know, but the experts are confident that it had to be a communal action. Once the pot was filled with coins, they used the upturned "dog dish" to make a lid, and this must have capped it off well.

The hoarders then carefully placed more lumps of the yellow clay around the lid, to stop it slipping, before putting on a covering with more clay until it came level with the rest. This then would have left a hole 3 feet across and about 12 inches deep. It would then have been an easy matter to fill in the top soil that they would have kept separate. Then, by removing the pile of clay that had not gone back into the hole, no sign would have been left for anybody to know just what had been going on. Did all this happen at night, so nobody else knew about what they had just done, or were they just confident that nobody would touch it, because it was a gift for the gods? That, archaeology cannot tell us!

Out of over 52,000 coins, only five were quality *denarii* silver coins - why? Were these coins from somebody who could afford that amount of money; were they making a point with their gods, or maybe just trying to impress the neighbours with their generosity?

Or were the *denarii* just dropped in there by mistake, just a slip of the fingers! I cannot see any Roman asking if he can get his five coins back because they were too valuable!

The Surrounding Area

There is no known villa activity anywhere close to the site, and no indication at all of a settlement in the area. Where the hoard was buried is close to where a Roman road crosses that part of Somerset, although its route is not known exactly. This was a major Roman artery from Salisbury in the east running to Charterhouse in the west. At the eastern end of this stretch of road was the Roman fort of Old Sarum (*Sorviodunum*), just outside modern Salisbury, which was an important encampment for the Romans. Charterhouse (*Iscalis*) was, in its own right, an important mineral resource area as it was a vital producer of lead, with silver as an important by-product. Salisbury was also a main road from London via Silchester which continued, via Dorchester, to the coast. This made the road a good way of transferring goods and people across the country. Just before reaching Charterhouse the road crossed the Fosse Way, another main Roman road, making this region a very accessible area to all travellers. There are many villas spread across this part of Somerset and Wiltshire, with many more yet to be found. There is also an important temple at Cold Kitchen Hill, on the road just by Maiden Bradley. So with all these factors, this gives us a well-used road passing close to the find spot. The people who passed on their travels included, primarily, the military forces that had the roads built for speedy communication and the movement of troops. In addition, there was the local and municipal administration - merchants with their wares, the postal system, and of course all the civilian population. This was a well-used and busy road.

Their Gods

The shape of this empty hole in 2010 told its own story; this was what the Somerset Romans had dug 1700 years ago to hide their offering for their gods. People in that time took their belief in the gods to the extreme; gods lived in the trees, the wind, the water, houses, and in the ground....in fact they had a god just about everywhere! It was a fundamental principle of their belief that if you made an offering, which could be coins, a brooch, a ring, a bracelet or just about anything that had value, then the gods would look favourably on the giver who would receive some benefit to themselves. This was their core pre-Christian belief. So by placing a valuable item into water, where it would disappear out of sight, the gods would accept the item, and would then help the giver with their problem. They even believed that writing a curse down against somebody else, and sending that with a gift, would bring hardship to that person.

This belief in their gods and that they could, by giving gifts, alter the natural world around them, seems to be the logical reason why the hoard was put there. They needed something in return; maybe they had had a few bad years with poor crops, or disease in their animals. Maybe they had experienced a few very dry years. Any of these would need a suitable offering. It would also seem logical that this vast amount of small change was not given by one person, but probably by a whole group or community, getting together to ask their gods for help.

The amount of trouble that they went to in order to bury this gift, and the fact that nobody came back to retrieve it, shows how they felt about their beliefs. I just hope that they got what they wanted, and the gods gave them better weather or better crops the following year. Perhaps that next year, AD 294 or 295, was a good sunny and moist year; perhaps they grew a bumper crop of cabbages, and this was all their profit. I do hope so!

Roger and Sam in the BM enjoying my presentation cabbage picture joke.

There was another reason that suggests they were not coming back for the coins, and that was that they had used a very deep pot with a narrow neck. So if they had wanted to retrieve the coins at some stage they would have had to break the jar in the hole to get at all the coins, with a fair chance of losing some. Also to dig out the pot would have taken as much, if not more, work as it took to bury it in the first place and, at 160kg, it would have been too heavy to lift.

Back to the present, it was then just a matter of me checking the hole to ensure there was nothing else buried there, or that any of the coins had been missed. Then everybody gave a hand to refill the hole and make good the grass turf. Before the hole was filled in I felt we should leave something as a token of respect for their beliefs so I threw in a handful of modern coins I had in my pocket, which included a couple of foreign ones saying, "That will flummox the archaeologists in a thousand years time!"

Not One Hoard, But Two!

The British Museum

A day later, Roger and Sam came all the way down from London to collect the coins, and only just managed to get all of them into their car! So off they went, back to the British Museum, to allow basic conservation on the coins to be be carried out as soon as possible. This consisted of carefully washing the coins, one bag at a time, then drying them separately laid out on large trays, to ensure they didn't stick together.

Each layer of coins, after being washed, was laid out individually for drying - all 52,000 of them.

It took about nine weeks, just to wash and stabilise them! They could then be counted, and sorted into different emperors. The coins in each numbered bag were washed, dried, sorted, and counted separately, to ensure they did not get mixed up. So even now they can fix any coin to a particular layer in a certain part of the pot, and understand how it relates to any other part of the hoard. This helped them to squeeze every last piece of information from the find.

For this we can thank Pippa Pierce, metals conservator and the team at the British Museum for, without their expertise, we would not have ended up with so many well-preserved coins. Overall, some 400 hours have gone into the work on the coins so far, with a lot more to come. Roger and Sam counted and sorted the majority of the coins and many other unnamed PAS staff and colleagues also helped with this mammoth task.

This is all a far cry from the 1978 Cunetio Hoard; those coins could not even be related to which container they came from! All the coins were just dug up and completely jumbled together. There was a large opened mouth pot and, apparently, a lead container and there was no attempt, at the time, by the detectorists to keep the coins separate. There was no thought about the knowledge that would be lost forever. So we cannot be sure which coins, and how many, were in each of the containers, or indeed how many coins were originally in the total hoard.

When the archaeologists went back to the Cunetio hole and did an excavation they found more loose coins that had just been left lying around, and some even still in the hole. The amount of information that was lost was immense. The finding of these two large hoards, separated by 33 years, show completely different ideas of how to correctly metal detect, and what you should do (and not do!) if you find something which is of real importance, and you just might!

Continuity

I am, and always will be, the finder of the Frome Hoard, but it has always belonged to the Romanised Somerset people. When this pot was buried, in AD 293/294, the Romans had been here for over 200 years in the form of military personnel, administrators, tradesmen, artisans, and civilians. All of these people, generations of Romans, intermingled with the local tribes. Some of them married native women, raising children, mixing the Roman and Celtic genes. The present people of Somerset are the descendants of those for whom the hoard was so important. So who better to have the responsibility of safeguarding the hoard for future generations?

That is why I am very pleased that the hoard is "coming home" and is going to be on display in Somerset's Taunton Museum where it will be on show for locals and visitors alike. Maybe a relative of one of those Romans will come and marvel at the display of these 3rd century coins, and the striking grey ware pot, not realising that maybe some of his or her ancestors had put it there!

All Finished?

So there it was: the coins had gone to the British Museum, the hole had been filled in, and everybody else had left the field, and then there was just me. It was a funny sort of feeling after everything that had gone on over the last three days. Now all I had to do was to close the gate and walk away - or so I thought. On Saturday I locked the gate and drove home, thinking that it was all over bar the shouting - but how wrong I was! It was not long before the Somerset FLO was in touch by e-mail and asking me about going public. This is the one thing I did not really want to do before the inquest, as I thought it, would be better if it all came out on the day. Of course, I really had no idea how big the media thing was going to get.

It was just then that a few rumours started circulating, on a forum page, about a big find of Roman coins in Somerset, and it was evident that somebody in the know was leaking hints. The crunch came when before my Wiltshire FLO, Katie Hinds, had been told that the first count had been done (and it was approximately 52,500 coins), it was already on the internet "as over 52,000". Somebody "in the know" in Somerset was passing on hints and starting a lot of speculation. I was lucky to have a friend who used the same forum, and he was able to play it all down. From then on nothing more emerged, so maybe the leaker had second thoughts. But at least nothing had got into the wider press; pillow talk is best left just there!

Geophysical Survey

It was about a week after the coins had gone that it was felt by the BM that a geophysical survey would be a good idea. My farmer friend was happy, as he wanted to know if there was any reason the coins were there, and I was happy for this to go ahead, as it would prove that there was no habitation in the immediate vicinity. You can often tell if a site has had any amount of habitation on it over a period of time as the soil changes its composition with all the added mineralisation.

Every one of my good Roman sites starts to chatter when you cross the unseen edge. Sometimes you can see that the soil changes colour, and there is a marked difference with the amount of very small pottery shards; but on this site there was nothing like that at all.

Part of the surveying equipment used for the geophysics of the site.

It was on the following Friday that a team came down from Bradford and, over the weekend, covered the whole area with their survey.

So what did they find? Nothing! There were no foundations of a villa, or any other buildings, a ditch, or a road - there was nothing at all! There was not a single indication that the Romans had ever been there, apart from one large pot of coins and (100 years later) a scattered hoard of *siliquae*! I was pleased that I had been proved right, but still a little disappointed that nothing at all was found.

Things for me went quiet then and all I could do was wait. Roger and Sam, from the BM were really good in keeping me up to date with what they were doing, which was sorting and counting the coins as fast as Pippa and the team cleaned and dried them.

Digging For Britain

Alice and myself on a filming day in Somerset.

Digging For Britain was a BBC series about archaeology, including some of the most recent important finds from metal detectorists. It was in late May when Roger Bland got in touch and said the BBC were making a pilot programme about Roman Britain for this new series, and would I like to be involved with the events surrounding the hoard? I said I would think about it, and I did, for about 10 seconds! Then it turned out the presenter was Dr. Alice Roberts, from the "Coast" (and much else), and that was an added bonus. It was a great few days as it gave me a chance to see how they put the programme together. Working with Alice, albeit in a very small way, was great and at the same time very interesting; being interviewed by her was fun as she has a good sense of humour. John, the producer, and his team were helpful throughout, and I was pleased with the results. Of course all this filming had to be kept quiet as well, as the BM wanted to make a controlled major announcement of the hoard.

Live TV

It was in July that the BM had sent the paperwork to inform the Coroner that an inquest would soon be needed for the two hoards, and from this point any attempt at secrecy went pear shaped.

Early in April when I had written to the Coroner and informed him of the finds, I had asked for no publicity until the day of the inquest. This is one of the things that I believed you could request.

It was in early July that I received a phone call that heralded the publicity explosion. I was told that the Coroner's Office had just released a press statement that they were going to hold an inquest into a major Roman coin hoard. This also included my name (so much for asking for no publicity!).

Within hours I was doing interviews for the evening news in my garden for the BBC and ITV. The first TV news I did was live, and I was talking to, and answering questions from, the news team in London, and being filmed in my garden. Isn't technology great? That was a little nerve-racking, and I even managed to call a

Roman radiate a radial! It's funny now but at the time I was cursing! The phone had started to ring and never seemed to stop. I went to work the next day but I never got much work done, or a moment's peace, as my unfortunate wife at home had to answer the phone all day, and pass on my number as everybody seemed to want know about the hoard on live radio. If it wasn't a local station somewhere in Great Britain, (and there's plenty of them), it was Canadian, or Australian radio. These interviews went on for about three weeks, and in the end I must have done about 40!

BBC and ITV Film crews parked outside the house; I'm glad the hedge was cut okay.

Field Day For The Papers

The next day the papers had a field day as everybody across the world knew about the hoard at the same time. It's a pity that they didn't all check their facts about the valuation procedure, but perhaps they all made inflated guesses to sell newspapers. The independent valuation by the Treasure Valuation Committee was months away, but that did not stop them being "creative" with what they thought it was going to be worth, with the *Daily Express* coming up with a silly figure of £3.3 million. Then it was a case of continuing my work with more interviews and rushing in and out of local studios.

Minted...the cook who found £3.3m of Roman coins in a farmer's field

By John Chapman

METAL detector enthusiast Dave Crisp has unearthed one of the largest finds of Roman coins in Britain, it was revealed yesterday.

Mr Crisp, 63, found more than 52,000 coins, which date from the 3rd century, buried in a field near Frome, Somerset.

The hoard – valued at £3.3million – was in a huge jar just over a foot below the surface.

Mr Crisp, a married hospital chef from Devizes, Wiltshire, told how his detector gave a "funny signal," prompting him to dig down through the soil.

"I put my hand in, pulled out a bit of clay and there was a little radial, a little bronze Roman coin. Very, very

Where do they get their information?

When it made the headlines in Australia, one of my great nephews, Peter from Coffs Harbour, was the toast of his school when he was able to tell them he was related to me (poor soul!).

The Inquest

The Coroner's Inquest, which is a legal formality, was to be held in Frome with a public display of some of the coins in the afternoon.

This was the first time the public had an opportunity to see any of the coins and was being held in Frome Library.

On the telly again.

The day started for me as I arrived driving past the court house, and saw the outside was packed with reporters and camera crews. It was a good start as the car park was full, and there was no parking on the road I had to drive around the corner and walk all the way back and, as I had cut the time short, and got besieged by questions on arrival, I only just made it in time!

The Coroner was nice chap and after he had heard Anna's bit, he asked me to take the stand, and tell my story as to how I found the hoard. It was all very laid back, and I found it a good laugh and not at all intimidating. He asked all the right questions, thanked me for my evidence, and then summed up all that he had heard, including the written evidence from Roger Bland and Sam Moorhead of the British Museum. As expected, he ruled that the hoard was Treasure and this was the only way it could have gone, being the obvious decision. Outside it was quite chaotic as the journalists, and a couple of TV reporters, all wanted quotes and interviews. I managed to get away in the end, and drove down into the town to the library.

Frome Library

As I parked one of my farmer friends met me and told me to hurry as the waiting queue was out into the car park! Interested people had started to arrive when the library opened, and only Sam was there as it wasn't supposed to start till lunchtime when we thought we would be finished with the inquest.

The people who came that day were enthusiastic and patient, as the queue was not moving very fast; in fact it didn't seem to be moving at all sometimes. I spent most of my time giving interviews, talking to people who were waiting in line, and explaining what I knew (very little then) about the coins. When I got home that night

Not One Hoard, But Two!

I was knackered, but was still on a high; the interest and enjoyment that people showed that day was quite wonderful.

That was an amazing day and some 2,000 people queued to see the coins. If you were one of them, I can only say thank you very much for coming, thank you for waiting in line, and I hope you thought it was worth the wait!

British Museum Display

It was late July that I received a phone call from my brother, up north, saying congratulations - he had seen the great coin display in the BM. I didn't even know there was one, but I quickly confirmed there was! My brother went on to say that he was very pleased for me, as I was the only person he knew of who had experienced a display in the British Museum, and wasn't even dead! I think it was a compliment, so I took it as one!

Frome open day - 2,000 local people queued to see just some of the coins.

Later I travelled up to London just to see what it was like. He was right; it was a great display in the middle of the long Roman room. I could not have wished for a better display or a better position for it.

I spent most of the day just standing there talking to people who stopped to admire the coins, and telling the story. I met a lot of good people that day, all interested and fascinated by the number of coins and the length of time they were in the ground.

The first display in the British Museum.

Frome Hoard Book

I was amazed when I first saw the book they had been written about the hoard. It was so well done: it told the basic story of the hoard, from the academic's point of view, and was an excellent account. In such a small book it managed to convey the context of the coins and what was happening at that time. It was written by Roger Bland and Sam Moorhead of the British Museum; Anna Booth who was the Somerset FLO, was there in late 2010 when there was book launch in a Bath Art Gallery, which Ann and Geoff, the landowners, and I attended. The authors were there and the manager from the printers who had done such a good job, in a very short time. The book gives such a wonderful insight into the coins of Carausius, and the time scale of the Roman Occupation.

The official Frome Hoard book, written by the experts.

The Landowners

No book on metal detecting would be complete unless the landowners and farmers were fully complimented and thanked for giving permission to complete strangers (in most cases) to park, walk across, and dig holes on their land. It takes a very agreeable sort of person to allow us access to their farm.

Ann and Geoff are two of these. I first knocked on their door in 2009 introducing myself as having permission to detect on their neighbour's farm, and that I was sure that the Romans had been in the area. I then said could I metal detect on their land as well, please? They were both charming, and interested in the history of the area. They realised that a Roman road crossed their land, but had never seen anything that might indicate habitation.

They both made me welcome, explaining they had given permission to a metal detectorist before, but nothing interesting had been shown to them. I assured them that they would be the first to know if I found anything. Little did we

Ann, Geoff and myself at the official book launch in Bath.

guess what was to come, just over 12 months later! So from all metal detectorists everywhere, many thanks to all the farmers and landowners who give permission and a special thank you to Ann and Geoff, shown here at the book launch held in Bath in 2010.

Treasure Valuation Committee

This is where the price is put on the hoard, or any other Treasure item. After the Coroner has declared the item (the hoard in this case) Treasure, the TVC can then go ahead and value it. This board is completely independent, and is made up of experts from various fields. They come from a variety of professions and they even have a metal detectorist on it, who is Trevor Austin, the General Secretary of the NCMD.

The committee asked two large auction houses to come in and put an estimated provisional valuation of what the hoard would fetch on the open market. They came to the BM on separate days and each valued the coins as to what they thought. A written valuation was received from each, but as they were so very different a third auction house was commissioned to do another. When this was received, the committee then used all three valuations as a basis to work from.

The committee members take these valuations and proceed to give their views on them, giving reasons, and considering any recent sales on similar items. After a discussion they come to a compromise valuation that everyone is happy with. It is apparent that they take the valuations seriously, and I personally believe that they do a sensitive job very professionally.

The announcement of the funding at the Museum of Somerset.

You are sent a provisional valuation letter before the committee sits, and it is at this stage you can comment on the estimate, and can still even have your own valuation done. Also, if you feel that there is not enough time for this you can request an adjournment to the next meeting. Indeed, I did once, a few years ago, ask them to take into consideration some further evidence on the valuation of a single item I had found, and the outcome was very favourable.

The Frome Hoard was valued at a total of £320,000, which was split 50/50 between the owner of the land and me. I was very pleased with this figure, as was the landowner, and I felt this was a fair valuation. It was actually more than I had estimated, but I did not have the specialised knowledge on the better quality coins that were mixed in with the rest, or the up-to-date prices that particular coins were getting in the auction houses.

With nearly all Treasure items, they are first offered to a local museum to purchase. If they want the item for their display, they have to raise the cash by asking charitable institutions for donations or using their own reserves. For the purchase of the Frome Hoard we shall always be indebted to the three main contributors: The National Heritage Memorial Fund, The Victoria and Albert Purchase Fund, and the Art Fund. Donations were also received from smaller institutions and some very generous individuals.

The Coins

Let's talk coins - all 52,503 of them! It was probably in AD 293 or early 294 that these sack loads of coins were deposited into the ground in modern Somerset. Why they were deposited, and why there, we shall talk about later. But we can make an educated guess as to when the coins were placed into the pot and buried, due to the type of coins. The latest coins are of Carausius and he was murdered in AD 293. So if there are no subsequent coins of any of his successors, then the chances are that it was buried late in 293, or very early in 294. The person who took over from Carausius, and made himself emperor, was another self-made man, Allectus (who was himself disposed of in 296 when Britain was taken back into the Roman fold).

Roman coins galore.
(Photo courtesy of Mike Hogan)

This is relevant because there were no coins of Allectus or any of the future emperors in the hoard. All that said, there are also still 8,000 coins that need conservation before they can be identified, so as they are cleaned any of the numbers or the dates may yet change!

Of the coins that we know so far, the vast majority of them are base metal silver radiates. Some are in better condition than others but the majority only have five percent (or less) of silver with the remainder being made up of various sorts of bronze. Some of the coins are just silver washed. Overall, the majority are in quite good condition, although the quality of some at the moment leaves a lot to be desired. It's going to be a long slow process to conserve all the coins, as they have to be done by hand one at a time. This is all so they can be preserved for future generations to see and study.

Well, as of now, we know that there are 20 emperors' coins in the pot plus those of a few wives, and a couple deified after their deaths. The range covered is between Valerian (AD 253), and Carausius (AD 293), so 40 years. The most of any one emperor is Tetricus who ruled in the period AD 271-274. The next highest amount is those of Victorinus (AD 269-271) with about 7,500 coins. The least any emperor had to his name was Lacelian who had only four coins, but as he seems to have managed not quite a year in the top job, this short stay might have something to do with it! Carus' wife did manage to get two into the pot, but Carus, himself only managed eight in his one year in the top job (AD 282-283). The ones of these that seemed to excite the academics most were the coins of Carausius, and there were nearly 800 of these and this raised a few eyebrows as it's the highest number of his coins ever found in one place. (See Sam Moorhead's piece on coin finds).

The initial washing and drying has stabilised the condition, but it is going to take a year or more for two people to properly clean and conserve each coin individually. With this will come a greater knowledge of the coins, and what was going on in this period.

With all these radiates there were just five coins that were truly exceptional. These were five silver *denarii*, in extraordinarily good condition. They did not appear to have any significant wear, suggesting that they were placed into the pot soon after they were minted.

A *denarii* is a Roman silver coin that had been produced and used by the Romans from the early years of their civilisation, and 25 of them was worth one gold *aureus* coin.

What made these coins exceptional was the fact they were minted in this country, and by the rebel emperor Carausius.

Carausius - Rebel, Usurper, Pirate and Lost Emperor

Carausius was apparently all of the above and more! He was born on the modern day Dutch/Belgium border, apparently of middle class parents. He joined the military and came up through the ranks, rising high enough to come to the attention of the emperor. He was then given a job as the commander of the Roman fleet in the channel to keep it free from Saxon and other raiders who were looting the coastal towns of Britannia, and threatening the grain and cargo ships that were crossing the channel for trade.

After a while it was alleged that he found it more profitable to intercept the raiders after they had plundered the coastal regions, and then to keep the spoils for himself. This might have all been conjecture, but when Maximian recalled him back to Rome he knew his time was up, and that if he went he wasn't coming back.

So he had little choice but to declare himself Emperor of Britain and part of Gaul and take his chances. Now at first this appeared to go okay. After all, he had command of the fleet in the channel, and a good power base in Gaul; so without a fleet and a base to attack from Maximian could not do much. The first thing Carausius needed to do was to tell everybody that he was the guy in charge, and he did this through his coins. He paid the army in Britain with coins that had his portrait and carried titles that seemed to give legitimacy to his rule, and this secured his position (a common ploy with Roman rulers). Carausius stayed in the job for seven years, quite a good run for a usurper who didn't have a claim to the title!

So why am I going on about him and his coins? Well, the five exceptionally rare silver *denarii*, which were found in the hoard, have on them some political quotations from Virgil (a literary poet who died in 19 BC). It was a bit like quoting Shakespeare today, a little OTT perhaps but Carausius used all this propaganda to give validity to his claim. The reverse graphics were also used to make a point. By including a picture of Romulus and Remus (the historical founders of Rome) feeding from the she wolf he was saying he was of the old school, and had strong links with Rome. The pair of clasped hands meant he was a good friend of the army, from where he came originally.

The bottom coin displays two standing figures, which represents the goddess Britannia greeting Carausius, which gives the message that he is welcome in Britain and is a good chap to have around.

"The golden age is back!" and "Come, awaited one!" were two

of the quotes he used on his coins, to put himself forward as the chosen person.

This is the tweeter; the face book of its time. This is how they told the people what they wanted them to know.

The illustration, right, shows him on a horse riding triumphantly, probably into London, and just speaks for itself. Hail the victor, hail the liberator! The present day spin doctors of government had nothing on this bloke!

These coins, as with all those issued by each emperor, are used to communicate with the people and troops; they are the text of their time, the e-mails to all and sundry. This was the information and propaganda that helped an emperor stay in power once he was there!

Unfortunately, like all men who hold power with the sword, the end is nearly always the same. Carausius had a finance minister by the name of Allectus and in AD 293 it was he who gained power over our man in the usual way. Carausius was assassinated, and Allectus took over, but only managed to hold the job down for just over two years. His time came to an end when Constantius managed to retake Britain for Rome in AD 296. By that time the hoard had already been in the ground for at least two years!

Along with these five silver *denarii* came nearly 800 radiates of Carausius. This is the largest single number of his coins ever found and will keep the academics happy for years to come. The knowledge that will be gained from this pot of coins will be incredible, and it will be studied for years.

Final Siliquae Count

I have now found just about 70 *siliquae* from the first hoard, made up of whole coins, broken bits, and bent coins. The condition of the coins is overall not too bad, but if you take away all the clipped and broken examples, it doesn't leave many in really top condition; but I was very pleased to find them! There is a photo of some of them at the beginning of the chapter, and I don't expect to find any more except when the field is ploughed in a few years' time, when I might come across a few bits and pieces. I am not finding any more now, so I expect that's it; still I can't complain, it wasn't a bad find! These 4th century AD coins must have been hidden in the early 390s, so that is just about 100 years after the big hoard. This was probably a hoard of coins that had been disturbed by the plough years ago, and has been spread across the field every time it was ploughed ever since. Anna Booth found a reference to some workers digging a ditch and finding some silver coins of the same type, in the same area of Somerset, in 1867. They may have found the bottom of the broken pot. All of these *siliquae* are of a fairly standard type, except one. This was a half *siliqua*, which are quite rare, with a picture of Roma on one side and a cross in a wreath on the other. The academics are still not completely sure what these half *siliqua* were for, or when they were made, but Roger Bland at the BM has written an article for the *Numismatic Chronicle*, making a good case for when and why.

Half *siliqua* showing the head of Roma.

My coin comes from the Trier mint, shown by the TR under the wreath. Trier is Germany's oldest city with Augustus establishing a base there in 16 BC, and it became a chosen city for many emperors after that. The picture of Roma is a standard portrait of the god of Rome. It seems likely that these small, rare coins were made just for a couple of particular occasions, like an emperor's anniversary celebration, and were made to be given away as a gift. Going on what Roger and Sam have indicated it would seem a late 4th century date, in the 390s, is more than probable.

Talks and The Japanese

Early on I was asked to do a short documentary for a Brazilian TV company (you know how it is!). Since then the hoard has continued to attract attention, with plenty of offers to give talks to clubs and historical societies that are still interested in the coins. I have also been privileged to help Roger and Sam, from the BM, to give their academic talks about the hoard and the coinage of the time. All of these talks have the theme of Roman Britain at the time of the hoard, and the link with Carausius in particular.

It was in late July 2011 that I had a call from ITV about doing an interview for a pilot show for a series on the PAS and metal detecting finds, and I did a day's filming. I must say they did a good lunch (with a little help from M&S!), but the rest of the day was a bit of a letdown; but you can't win them all! I was also lucky to help with a Japanese short documentary about metal detecting and we did this filming at a rally near Tiverton. It was a good weekend where a lot of our club members came and camped, and we had a good two days' detecting; it was just a pity that decent finds were nonexistent! This left me with plenty of time for filming on the Saturday. It was shown on a Japanese late night show, but I never did manage to see it. What they wanted it for, still beats me, maybe it was a sketch thing, like Benny Hill!

Not One Hoard, But Two!

Back Home!

It was on 29 September 2011 that some of the hoard came back to Somerset, after its short visit to London. It is now housed in the Museum of Somerset, which is in the newly refurbished Taunton Castle. This building has been closed for two years and they have spent £6.5 million on this revamp, which has produced a really great backdrop for the hoard. This is now a really modern museum that is certainly worth a visit, and would make a great day out for all the family. It is also free to get in and there is a small modern café, which serves snacks and good coffee, with outside summer seating.

The coins' new home in Taunton Somerset.

They have put the large pot back together. I suppose for the staff at the British Museum it was just like a large jigsaw (all you needed was a bit of superglue and a lot of patience!). They must have been really pleased how carefully Alan Graham had taken it apart, kept it all separate, and well-marked, as he dismantled it piece by piece.

So what we have now is the pot fully restored, seemingly full with coins right to the top; with the upside down black burnished ware "dog dish", sitting just above it like a hat. A lot of the nice dark colour has now gone from the pot, and it has returned to its probable original colour, which was just a dry-looking grey. They don't call this type of Roman pottery grey ware for nothing!

The display of some of the coins with the upside down "dog dish" as a hat.

Round the base there are scattered a couple of hundred of the radiates, which are all they have in the museum at the moment. The

The display in its temporary setting in the Museum of Somerset, Taunton.

five exceptional silver *denarii* take pride of place, on their own little plinth on the left. Around the glass display cabinet on the three sides are the stories, in photos, of the coins and a little of the excavation, with some of the people involved.

This is only the first large display of the hoard in its new home in Somerset. The majority of the coins are still being cleaned and conserved in London and this is an ongoing job with two conservators working full time to get this work done. It is still going to take 18 months, as it's a very slow process. Each coin has to be worked on individually, so they are in a condition that will last. As the museum receives more of the conserved coins back from the BM, the display will, I am sure, get bigger and better.

Slightly Technical Bit

On the day I found the large hoard I was using my excellent Minelab Explorer II detector. I had bought this off the Internet, and paid less than half price for a "nearly new" one. This detector has now served me well for a few years, and is still going fine. I have a deep and fast program on it, which Mick Turrell kindly set up for me a couple of years ago at a rally, and I have never found a reason to change it. You have to get used to a little chatter as, if you are on a good site, it picks up everything; but you do know you are not missing anything if you pass over it.

The signal on that day was iffy; on another day, and not looking for those little cut bits of *siliquae*, I might not have stopped and dug; and that's quite a sobering thought!

Would I have found this hoard with one of my other two detectors (old but still serviceable)? No, I don't believe I would have, the top of the pot was just too deep.

Summing Up

So that's about it for this story. From that first day in April 2010, when I just went out for a day's detecting, through the initial discover, the three day excavation, and all the wonderful people who have been involved right through the last two years. This includes all the people who have helped me and have been involved with the coins at the British Museum, the two excellent FLOs, the new Somerset Museum personnel; and Alan Graham, the private archaeologist, who re-established my belief in archaeology! To all these people I would like to say thank you, you all did a fantastic job and I would not be writing this book without the help you willingly gave to the hoard and myself.

So with 52,500 Roman coins under my belt, this means I am still the finder of the largest single hoard of Roman coins ever, and I will be till somebody, somewhere finds another bigger one. Is there another one out there? Well yes there must be, but was there a pot made larger than the Frome one? Who knows, but when it is found, I am sure it will be a metal detectorist who finds it.

It has been a fantastic two years. I never did get to detect on that ploughed field in Somerset, but that field will still be there for me next year, or the year after.

I hope everybody has enjoyed reading about my find, and if it starts some people taking up detecting correctly then I have achieved with this book what I set out to do.

The Treasure Act

A summary of the Treasure Act 1996, and the Extension of January 2003

All finders of gold and silver objects, and groups of coins from the same finds, over 300 years old, have a legal obligation to report such items under the Treasure Act 1996. Now prehistoric base-metal assemblages, found after 1st January 2003, also qualify as Treasure.

What objects qualify as Treasure in England, Wales and Northern Ireland?

1. Any metallic object, other than a coin, provided that at least 10 per cent by weight of metal is precious metal (that is, gold or silver) and that it is at least 300 years old when found. If the object is of prehistoric date it will be Treasure provided any part of it is precious metal.

2. Any group of two or more metallic objects of any composition of prehistoric date that come from the same find (if found after 1 January 2003).

3. All coins from the same find provided they are at least 300 years old when found (but if the coins contain less than 10 per cent of gold or silver there must be at least ten of them). Only the following groups of coins will normally be regarded as coming from the same find:
   - Hoards that have been deliberately hidden
   - Smaller groups of coins, such as the contents of purses that may have been dropped or lost
   - Votive or ritual deposits.

4. Any object, whatever it is made of, that is part of the same find as another object that is Treasure. An object or coin is part of the "same find" as another object or coin if it is found in the same place as, or had previously been together with, the other object. Finds may have become scattered since they were originally deposited in the ground.

5. Any object that would previously have been Treasure-trove, but does not fall within the specific categories given above. Only objects that are less than 300 years old, that are made substantially of gold or silver, that have been deliberately hidden with the intention of recovery and whose owners or heirs are unknown will come into this category.

Under the Treasure Act 1996 there is a legal obligation to report all finds of Treasure within 14 days from when they become aware that the item might be Treasure.

The National Council for Metal Detecting

The National Council for Metal Detecting Code of Conduct

1. Do not trespass. Obtain permission before venturing on to any land.
2. Respect the Country Code, leave gates and property as you find them and do not damage crops, frighten animals or disturb nesting birds.
3. Wherever the site, do not leave a mess or an unsafe surface for those who may follow. It is perfectly simple to extract a coin or other small object buried a few inches below the ground without digging a great hole. Use a suitable digging implement to cut a neat flap (do not remove the plug of earth entirely from the ground), extract the object, reinstate the grass, sand or soil carefully, and even you will have difficulty in locating the find spot again.
4. If you discover any live ammunition or any lethal object such as an unexploded bomb or mine, do not disturb it. Mark the site carefully and report the find to the local police and landowner.
5. Help keep Britain tidy. Safely dispose of refuse you come across.
6. Report all unusual historical finds to the landowner, and acquaint yourself with current NCMD policy relating to the Voluntary Reporting of Portable Antiquities.
7. Remember it is illegal for anyone to use a metal detector on a designated area (e.g. scheduled archaeological site, SSSI, or Ministry of Defence property) without permission from the appropriate authority.
8. Acquaint yourself with the definitions of the following documents:-
   (1) Treasure contained in the Treasure Act 1996 and its associated Code of Practice, making sure you understand your responsibilities.
   (2) Advice for Finders of Archaeological Objects including Treasure 2006.
9. Remember that when you are out with your metal detector you are an ambassador for our hobby. Do nothing that might give it a bad name.
10. Never miss an opportunity to explain your hobby to anyone who asks about it.

Appendix A to the NCMD Constitution,
Revised February 2000,
Amended AGM June 2007

Trevor Austin. NCMD General Secretary.
51 Hilltop Gardens, Denaby, Doncaster. DN12 4SA
Tel: 01709 868521

National
Council
for
Metal Detecting

NCMD
NATIONAL COUNCIL FOR METAL DETECTING
TO PROMOTE
TO PROTECT
TO ENCOURAGE

Member of: The Sport and Recreation Alliance

MODEL SEARCH AGREEMENT

I...being the owner / occupier of land premises

known as...situated at..

agree that in consideration of the payment to the landowner / occupier of...........% of the value or rewards arising from the recovery of any property or objects found by the undersigned [herein after called the licensee(s)] over the value of £ .... , the licensee(s) may enter the said land or part thereof to search for items of buried or other material, whether antique or modern.

This agreement shall continue in force from (date) ....until (date). ....
Provided that: -
1 The licensee(s) shall hold a current NCMD membership card showing, details of their £10,000,000 Public Liability Insurance cover.

2. The licensee(s) shall always observe and adhere to the Code of Conduct as set out by the NCMD which is a condition of membership and includes reference to the voluntary Code of Practise for Responsible Metal Detecting (See overleaf).

3. The licensee(s) shall strictly observe and adhere to any guidelines or special conditions and area boundaries, which may be set out by the owner / occupier from time to time and to any terms and conditions with respect to metal detecting access specified in agri -environment agreements which may cover all or part of the said land.

4. The licensee(s) shall record finds made on the said land with third parties including The Portable Antiquities Scheme (PAS), Historic Environment Records (HER) or any museum service only after gaining the appropriate permission of the landowner to do so and then only to an accuracy of findspots that all parties are comfortable with. All parties must abide by the terms and conditions of any agri-environment schemes that specify mandatory reporting of all finds made on land covered by such agreements with the PAS. *(Agri-Environmental Schemes are not applicable to Scotland and Wales*)

Special conditions and boundaries,

....

....

Signed ....Owner / occupier Date................................

Signed ....Licensee Date ....

Name ....

Address..

Available to download from www.ncmd.co.uk

Appendix 3

Further Reading

For some of you, this book will be all you will ever feel the need to read but, hard though it is to believe, there is even more knowledge out there than we've been able to cram in! So if you want to find out more about a topic here are some of the books that we think you will find useful.

Chapter 9: Coins

Celtic Coins

Ancient British Coins published by Chris Rudd (www.celticcoins.com). At £75 ABC is pricey but it is the comprehensive guide to the subject; if you can't afford it personally, get your club to buy it!

Roman Coins

Coinage of Roman Britain by Richard Reece, published by Tempus 2002 (ISBN 0-7524-2523-4).

Anglo-Saxon Coins

Early Anglo-Saxon Coins by Gareth Williams, published by Shire Publications 2008 (ISBN 978-0-7478-0680-6). Interesting, and well-illustrated volume but it stops at Alfred.

General Coins

Coins of England 47th edition, published by Spink 2012 (standard catalogue, updated annually, and frankly, a "must have").

General Coins

England's Striking History ed. by C. H. Perkins, published by Rotographic 2006 (ISBN 0-948964-85-5). A very readable book on hammered coins - excellent sketches.

Chapter 10: Artefacts

Buckles

Buckles by Ross Whitehead, published by Greenlight 2003 (ISBN 1-897738-17-X). Lots of examples shown - puts your buckles into context!

Buttons

Metal Buttons 900BC-1700AD by Brian Read, published by Portcullis 2005 (ISBN 0-9532450-4-7). The definitive book, but sadly leaves out the 18th and 19th centuries.

Coin Weights

Lion Ships and Angels by P. & B.R. Withers, 2nd edition published by Galata 2011 (ISBN 978-1-908715-00-5). Not cheap, but it is the definitive work and used by FLOs!

Roman Artefacts

Roman Dress Accessories by Ellen Swift, published by Shire Publications 2003 (ISBN 0-7478-0567-9). Good on brooches, but covers other things too.

Tokens

Tokens & Tallies by Edward Fletcher, published by Greenlight 2003 (ISBN 1-897738-161). A useful overview - lots of photos.

Pottery

Pottery in Britain, 4000 BC to AD 1900 by Lloyd Laing, published by Greenlight 2003 (ISBN 1-897738-145). Useful introduction to styles.

General Artefacts

Archaeological Finds by Norena Shopland, published by Tempus 2005 (ISBN 0-7524-3132-3). Does some things, like Roman brooches, very well but patchy.

Benet's Artefacts 2nd edition, published by Paul Murawski 2003 (ISBN 0-9536172-1-1). Another "must have" and a lavishly illustrated guide, with values.

The Handbook of British Archaeology by Roy & Lesley Adkins & Victoria Leitch, published by Constable 2008 (ISBN 978-1-84529-606-3-9). Very useful for understanding finds in context.

Chapter 11: PAS and Treasure

A Decade of Discovery published by Archaeopress 2010 (ISBN 978-1-4073-0723-7). A collection of academic papers presented at a PAS conference in 2007 to mark its first decade and to show the use made of the database.

Chapter 12: Conservation and Cleaning

Conservation Advice Notes published by the PAS 2005 (ISBN 1-874454-34-5). Free!

Conservation for Metal Detectorists by Richard Hobbs, Celia Honeycombe and Sarah Watkins, published by Tempus 2002 (ISBN 0-7524-2522-6). Comprehensive and a good read, if you like this sort of thing.

Chapter 13: Upgrading Later

Advanced Detecting by Norfolk Wolf, published by Greenlight 2005 (ISBN 1-897738-250). One to read after a few years' detecting - not before!

Chapter 14: Frome and Other Hoards

Life and Letters on the Roman Frontier by A.K. Bowman, published by BM press (ISBN-10 0415920256). Read what the Romans wrote. A great read.

The Frome Hoard by Sam Moorhead, Anna Booth and Roger Bland, published by the BM Press 2010 (ISBN 978-0-7141-2334-9). A great little book.

The Staffordshire Hoard by Kevin Leahy and Roger Bland, published by the BM Press 2009 (ISBN 978-0-7141-2328-8).

The Vale of York Hoard by Gareth Williams and Barry Ager, published by the BM Press 2010 (ISBN 978-0-7141-1818-5).

Roman Britain by Richard Hobbs & Ralph Jackson, published by the BM Press 2010 (ISBN 978-0-7141-5061-1). Excellent illustrations of Roman items.

Appendix 4

Useful Contacts

NCMD (National Council of Metal Detecting) www.ncmd.co.uk/
Membership Secretary, John Rigby Email: jjrigby@sky.com
6 Arkholme Ave, Blackpool, Lancs FY1 6QJ
NCMD General Secretary, Trevor Austin, 51 Hilltop Gardens, Denaby, Doncaster, DN12 4SA. Tel: 01709 868521

Trowbridge Metal Detecting Club www.trowbridgemdc.co.uk

Portable Antiquities Scheme http://finds.org.uk/

British Museum http://www.britishmuseum.org/

Crown Estate Land www.thecrownestate.co.uk/metal-detecting

Port of London Authority, London River House, Royal Pier Road, Gravesend, DA12 2BG.

Receiver of Wreck Tel: 02380 329 474 www.rats.ukdiver.com/wrecks/receiver.htm
105 Commercial Road, Southampton, SO15 1EG.
Email: row@mcga.gov.uk

Environment Agency http://www.ntenvironment.com/

Forestry Commission www.forestry.gov.uk/

Google Mapping site http://wtp2.appspot.com/wheresthepath.htm

The Laws in Northern Ireland Tel: 028 9054 3001 www.ehsni.gov.uk

The Laws in Scotland www.treasuretrovescotland.co.uk
info@treasuretrovescotland.co.uk

Metal Detecting Dealers (Moving roughly South to North!)

Detector Distribution Ltd Unit 5, Orchard Business Park, North End Road, Yapton, West Sussex BN18 0GA.
Tel: 01243 558899 and Website: www.detector-distribution.co.uk

Detecnicks Ltd 3 Orchard Crescent, Arundel Road, Fontwell, West Sussex BN18 0SD.
Tel: 01243 545060 and E-mail: sales@detecnicks.co.uk Website: www.detecnicks.co.uk

Joan Allen Electronics Ltd 190 Main Rd, Biggin Hill, Kent TN16 3BB.
Tel: 01959 571255 and E-mail: sales@joanallen.co.uk Website: www.joanallen.co.uk

Leisure Promotions The Kennet Centre, Newbury, Berkshire RG14 5EN.
Tel: 01635 46040 and Website: www.leisure-promotions.co.uk

Sunbury Detector Centre 1 Templedene Avenue, Staines, Middlesex TW18 1LH.
Tel: 01784 451678 and E-mail: sales@sunburydetectorsdirect.co.uk
Website: www.sunburydetectorsdirect.co.uk

Regton Ltd 82 Cliveland Street, Birmingham B19 3SN.
Tel: 0121 359 2379 Website: www.regton.com

Mike Longfield Detectors 83 Station Rd, Balsall Common, Coventry CV7 7FN.
Tel: 0800 435 097 and Website: www.metaldetectors.gbr.cc

Treasureland 598 Melton Rd, Thurmaston, Leicester LE4 8BB.
Tel: 0116 266 4012 and E-mail: sales@detectorland.co.uk
Website: www.detectorland.co.uk

Crawfords Detectors F6 Mercia Way, Foxhills Industrial Estate, Scunthorpe, North Lincolnshire DN15 8RE. Tel: 01724 845608 and E-mail: sales@crawfordsmd.co.uk
Website: www.crawfordsmd.co.uk

Pepsi Piro's Detectors 10 Carlton Rd, Worksop, Notts S80 1PH.
Tel: 01909 476611

Highland Innovation Centre Ltd 16 Blackpark Terrace, Inverness IV3 8NE.
Tel: 01463 222911 and E-mail: david@highland-innovation.com
Website: www.scottishmetaldetectors.com

Manufacturers' Contact Details (In alphabetical order)

C.Scope International Ltd Kingsnorth Technology Park, Wotton Rd, Ashford, Kent TN23 6LN. Tel: 01233 629181 and E-mail: info@cscope.co.uk
Website: www.csmetaldetectors.com

Garrett Website www.garrett.com

Minelab Tel: 0800 056 4246 and Website: www.minelab.com

Viking Metal Detectors Ltd 1 Angela Street, Mill Hill, Blackburn, Lancashire BB2 4DJ. Tel: 01254 55887 and E-mail: viking@metaldetectors.co.uk
Website: www.metaldetectors.co.uk

White's 35 Harbour Rd, Inverness, IV1 1UA.
Tel: 01463 223456 and E-mail: sales@whites.co.uk Website: www.whites.co.uk

XP Website: www.xpmetaldetectors.com

Appendix 5

Grid References

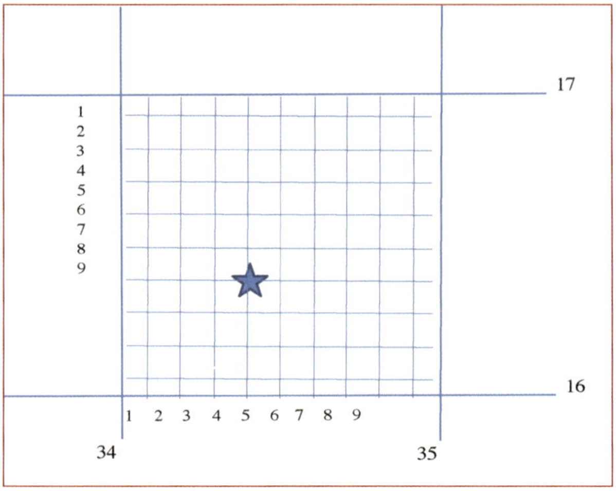

How To (Easily) Fix A Grid Reference

You have just made a good find that is worth recording, so you would like to show where you found it and give it a grid reference. This can then also be used to record your finds with the PAS. I find the best map to use is the Explorer OS (orange) series, which show field boundaries and have a 1:25,000 scale.

Each map has unique letters (i.e. SU), printed in the information section on the right hand side of the map, or in all four corners. This will be the first part of your grid reference.

The map squares represent a kilometre (1000m) square. You could just give a four figure grid reference, which simply says in which square km the object was found. The phrase to remember is "bottoms up!" meaning that you start with the numbers along the bottom (giving East-West) and finish with the numbers going upwards (North-South). So here it would be SU 34 16.

Yet this is not very accurate, and the PAS (rightly) prefer a more detailed reference (although this is withheld from the public). So the trick is to imagine each square is split into tenths. You can then estimate the nearest tenth and put that in the reference. So, in our example above, the six figure grid reference becomes SU 344 166, and this now pins our find to a square of only 100m sides.

Of course, a GPS reading will be more accurate still! There is also a very good site called "magic" where you can get a grid reference: www.magic.gov.uk/

Follow the link to map, click on interactive map, then the demonstration map. Use bottom left icons to move to your area/field. Click on top left hash (it will change to red).

Click pointer on your find area, and you can read off the grid reference.

Notes